The Conversion
of a Psychic

Books by Susy Smith

The Conversion
of a Psychic

~~~~~~~~

by Susy Smith

Doubleday & Company, Inc.
GARDEN CITY, NEW YORK
1978

The biblical quotations in this book are, in large part, from the New American Bible. Quotations are also used from Good News for Modern Man, the King James translation of the Bible, The Living Bible, and the Revised Standard Version.

ISBN: 0-385-12638-7
Library of Congress Catalog Card Number 76-50790

Copyright © 1978 by Susy Smith
ALL RIGHTS RESERVED
PRINTED IN THE UNITED STATES OF AMERICA
FIRST EDITION

Contents

The Conversion of a Psychic

CHAPTER I

"Come On In and Share My Happiness"*

"I must be going crazy," I thought, for words were being spoken in my mind that I was not originating.

"Yes, you are," said this voice inside my head. And then it took up a refrain and chanted it over and over again: "Susy's going crazy. Susy's going crazy."

For over a year I had been endeavoring to communicate with the spirits of the dead, and this is where it got me. Suddenly, somehow, an unknown force was crowding in on me and trying to take me over.

"Is it possible to become insane in just one area and still be okay in every other way?" I wondered, for my thinking processes were perfectly normal. Back then, in 1956, I knew nothing about possession or the possible danger of having my consciousness completely obliterated by malevolent entities when I unwittingly invited them in. Thank God, I evaded that, and my paths eventually led me to Christ. But so many others have tragic experiences when they attempt to become involved with spirit communication that it seems important to tell what happened to me as a warning of how *not* to proceed, as well as to share the ultimate joy that has come to me through my religion.

* Matt. 25:21 (Good News for Modern Man)

What happened to me is a long story: the story of my life, actually. It all began, the first time, when I was born, and the second time, when I was "born again."

Receiving the Baptism in the Holy Spirit can be the culmination of a long and difficult career of searching and seeking, as it was in my own case. Or it can happen quickly and easily to someone who has never once quarreled with ideologies or philosophical or religious theories. Perhaps it is even more meaningful when it comes to an older person who has endured as much from life as I have. I hope others who argue will be given something of value for their own seeking when they read about what I went through in my search and how I was ultimately captured by the Christianity I had shunned for so long. Believe me, there are better ways to learn to become a Christian than the long road I traveled. But even the way I did it is preferable to not ever attaining it at all. The goal is worth any effort, for I can now say, with St. Paul, that in union with Christ I have become rich in all things.

A friend who knew many of the details of my existence when I was a young woman once said to me, "Susy, for a girl who has been so sheltered, you have certainly had a lot of vicissitudes." I agreed with her, except that my life had not been all that sheltered, if the truth were known. While suffering through it, I have had numerous amorous capers, a great deal of travel, and the opportunity to make many wonderful friends, so there are no complaints about the over-all picture. Since 1955, much of my activity has been mental, and that's when the main trouble began. I was very fortunate to have managed to come out on top of it with at least enough philosophy to carry me at that time. I am well aware how close I came to being a candidate for an institution with rubber walls.

When quite young, I had given Christianity a real fight and then dismissed it from my reckoning and became an agnostic. Later I proceeded with a survey of other religious, philosophical, and metaphysical concepts. I have spent most of the past twenty-three years researching and writing in the psychic field, having published books about everything from ESP to ghosts to spirit communication. As I had more and more experiences, ranging from the ineffectual to the outright frightening —most especially the terror of fighting against the bad guys in my mind—I grew to realize that admonitions against such dabbling in the paranormal should be given, and so I exposed my soul, you might say, in *Confessions of a Psychic*. The many letters, of gratitude for my warnings, received from readers have proved that it was helpful.

When I finally came to Christianity, I was a relatively passive individual who did not know what she was missing. I was no longer urgently seeking answers to life's questions, believing I had found them to my intellectual satisfaction and that they were good. I had long before overcome the anguish of the intruding voices in my mind and had learned how to control any adverse factions of that nature. I had become convinced of the possibility of a life hereafter and so was no longer afraid to die. In a way, I almost looked forward to it. I was a positive thinker who loved God in my own, rather ambiguous style; but, to me, Jesus Christ was no more than an admirable historical figure of great beauty and love. I did not know the jubilation of sharing my life with Him.

Twenty-six of my books had been published, and I had just returned from a lecture tour on which the celebrity treatment was accorded me everywhere among those in the psychic field. So I felt myself to be reasonably successful—certainly as successful as I ever hoped or needed to be. I was looking forward to retirement in June 1976, when I would be sixty-five, feeling that what I was supposed to do with my life had been accomplished, that most of my songs had been sung.

And then the Lord reached out and grabbed me! That is the only way I can describe what happened to me and has continued to happen ever since.

In late February 1975 in Tucson, Arizona, where I now reside, Fay Peters, a member of my meditation class, mentioned that a friend had written to her about the charismatic renewal in the Christian church, saying that she had attended retreats at Picture Rocks, near Tucson, that had changed her life. This was the first time I had heard of this movement.

Two days later, my editor at Chilton called to say that they would publish a projected book of mine to be called *How to Achieve a Miraculous Healing.* He then asked, "Have you ever heard of Catholic charismatic renewal healing?" I said, "Yes, just barely." He said, "Well, the publisher is Catholic, and he wants a chapter on that in your book if it's all right with you." I said, "Sure."

The next morning's newspaper carried an announcement of a Catholic charismatic renewal retreat at Picture Rocks the following weekend—February 28 to March 2. At this time I thought all this was mere coincidence; but, for the sake of the book on healing, I decided to go, and Fay accompanied me. I arrived at the retreat with notebook and pencil in my purse and tape recorder slung over my shoulder, in order to gather material for the chapter for the new book. But, almost immediately, Fay and I were in the midst of such an unusual amount of love and joy that it engulfed us like a shining cloud. There was peace such as I had never known and, suddenly, the realization that this was what my life was really missing.

Picture Rocks, about fifteen miles northwest of Tucson, sits on a hillside in the midst of the Tucson Mountains, with a magnificent view across the valley, where the lights of the city glow at night. It is run by the Guadalupe League of the Redemptorist Order for the purpose of allowing people to get away and become closer to God without the distractions of home and family and work. Its physical plant consists of a chapel, meeting rooms, cafeteria, and dormitories, which are filled each weekend by groups of from twenty-five to fifty holding interdenominational retreats or seminars of one kind or another and soaking up the peaceful atmosphere.

"This is for everybody—a place to come and put things together," says Rev. James (Jim) Farrell, the director. "Everybody who comes here is part of our family. We want to instill the family spirit."

The chapel takes full advantage of the desert scenery, the

north and south walls being composed of rows of floor-to-ceiling windows that bring the spiny ocotillo and the saguaro and the twittering birds from the landscape into the room itself. Over the altar, on the west wall (which is made of rough-surfaced rock), is a large crucifix carved from native wood. In gold letters on this rocky wall are the words: "The Desert will lead you to your heart where I will speak."

Picture Rocks is indeed a restful place to listen for His words, and four or five charismatic renewal retreats are held there yearly, led by various Catholic priests. Our leader was Father Richard Schiblin, director of the Holy Redeemer Center, in Oakland, California.

Friday evening, the first session started in the assembly room. The initial activity consisted of much enthusiastic singing of simple little religious songs. If they had a lively beat, there was usually clapping in time to the music. Father Dick gave an introductory talk; then we sat quietly for a time. Occasionally someone said softly, "Praise the Lord" or "Praise You, Jesus," perhaps raising one arm or both in supplication. Except for the masses, which were to follow, there was very little Catholic ritual, nothing being formalized as in church services.

After a while, we went into the chapel to continue our worship. At that time, each of us was asked to introduce himself to his neighbor on the right and then stand up and tell what he had learned about him and his background.

Of course, Fay and I, having been attending a Religious Science church, announced ourselves as metaphysicians, having no idea that some of our new friends immediately labeled us as misguided souls who were into "occultism," which they equated with being "of the Devil." I even told Father Dick that his lecture on Friday night about the healing of memories was pure Science of Mind. He rather flinched. But even though many members of the group thought we had a lot to learn, and were praying for our salvation, they could not love us enough or do enough for us. Since I was on crutches at the time for my arthritic knees, there was always someone to carry my tray in the cafeteria, and someone else to hold doors open for me, and all the other little courtesies so often overlooked by many people.

Occasionally during the services, someone spoke in tongues, but it was more or less a private affair, the words being muttered or whispered rather than shouted. The thing that impressed me most was *chanting* in tongues, which was done fairly often during the seminar, under Father Dick's leadership. During this, the voices blended together harmoniously into an inspiring eulogy, as each person sang out certain sounds and syllables that had no identifiable meaning. Father Schiblin explained this chanting to me later as "simply exulting in the Lord, in the tradition of the Gregorian chant."

A healing service concluded the first evening's program, and I was one of the ones to receive attention. All the twenty-five persons present gathered around me, some holding hands in a circle and some with their hands on my head and shoulders as I sat on a chair in the center. As they prayed and chanted in tongues, tears began to pour from my eyes. I felt that I simply had to be healed, just because they all wanted it so much. And it is possible that a gastric condition was healed at that time, because I have felt better internally since then. Unfortunately, my painful joints continued on their merry way.

Fay and I were allowed to attend all the masses as well as the meetings during which there were no special ceremonies. We pointed out to Father Dick that we were not Catholic, but he said that if we accepted Jesus as our Savior that was enough. Having respected and loved Christ for a long while as the greatest, wisest, and most spiritually beautiful Man Who ever lived, I was so charged up by the electricity of love pervading the group that I was willing to add a new dimension to my regard for Him, for the time at least. And so with that attitude I found the masses beautiful.

On these occasions, several times someone stood up and spoke loudly and firmly in tongues, and then someone else arose and seemed to reply in English. I was to learn that this is called "interpretation," and it is the companion gift that must be sought along with speaking in tongues. The interpretation purports to give the content of what was just said in tongues; but, curiously enough, the interpreter does not understand what he is saying, either. He just feels impelled to rise and start talking, and when he does the words pour forth in English.

It was in this way that a prophecy came concerning me, but I was so unaware of what was actually going on that I had no idea it referred to me. Later, two different people spoke to me of the prophecy, which they called a "double prophecy," because it had two parts. It was to this effect, as nearly as they remembered: "It shall come to pass that you will write on behalf of the Lord Jesus," and "I will light up your life." I knew the last part was true even before leaving the seminar.

I was later to learn that not only was there a prophecy about my writing this book, but there were prayers for it as well. As we introduced ourselves to our neighbors that first night, on my right was Virginia Bache of Phoenix, whose face truly glowed with the love of the Lord. I told her I was an author of psychic books and she immediately started praying that I would write a book for Jesus, and she kept up her prayers even after the retreat was over. I did not know this until we got together for luncheon a year and a half later and I told her my book was under way.

During our workshop period on Saturday afternoon, we were asked to write out our covenants with God. I gave my reaction to the whole experience in mine:

> My covenant is to try in the future in my life to reveal the wonderful qualities of love and faith that I have seen exhibited here this weekend. If I can do it within the framework that I have been operating in, well and good. If I have to change and open up more to some of the challenging ideas with which I have here been presented—well, my life has always been dedicated to growing and learning spiritually. I won't stop now.

I added a P.S.: "I hereby dedicate my life to God and to Jesus Christ as He epitomizes Love and the Resurrection, which is my special interest."

Although at that time I did not understand or condone the idea of communion, at the Eucharist service Saturday night I accepted the wafer and the wine as an act of commitment to Jesus. I wanted somehow to tell Him that I loved Him and to thank Him for those wonderful people. Actually I made a pledge to Him, although I wasn't clear about what it was. The longing for the same kind of rapport with Jesus that these others had, had somehow affected me, and I wanted to learn to know Him and to love Him as they did.

In the May 1972 issue of the *Full Gospel Business Men's Voice*, Marvin Aranove says, in "Hebrew of the Hebrews—The Story of a Fulfilled Jew": "It wasn't the impressive church on the corner that won me to Jesus, because I would never, under my own impetus, have walked in. Nor was it an eloquent and persuasive preacher, because I wouldn't have listened. It wasn't the fear of hell or the desire to go to heaven that won me to Jesus. *It was the love manifested in those lives that had touched mine that made me hungry for what they had.*"

This was my exact reaction, and being the kind of person I am, I did not stop until this hunger was satisfied.

CHAPTER II

"...Those Who Sit in Darkness and in the Shadow of Death..."*

The kind of person I am was undoubtedly initiated by my Scotch and German forebears on Mother's side and English and French-Canadian on my father's. Unless some fey and romantic Scot got in there, they were probably all of relatively prosaic natures. There were no highwaymen that I know of, but Daddy had an ancestor who fought under Roger Williams, the founder of Rhode Island.

My parents could be described as rather sensible people of character and good will. Daddy was a constant reader, and I acquired that trait from him. Mother was not a reader but a doer. With a disposition to match her gorgeous auburn hair, she was the most determined individual I've ever encountered, and some of that certainly got into my blood. You could almost call me stubborn when I set my mind to accomplishing something.

It seems wise to indicate that I had a relatively sound heritage, because one who trucks with the unknown as much as I have can easily be dismissed as a kookie-bird whose testimony is of no value. What is in my mind instead is to suggest that, coming of good stock, I became a fairly well adjusted adult who was probably strengthened by all the rebuffing experiences and serious illnesses of my life and so was better able to keep

* Luke 1:79 (New American Bible)

from breaking down under the violent mental pressure that occurred later, when the time came for my attempts to communicate with spirits.

Analyzing the person I became, it seems to me that I am a levelheaded individual with very little imagination and a lot of self-discipline and common sense. One of my main characteristics is argumentative reasoning. I know my most continuous and most aggravating phrase all through my childhood was "Why, Daddy?" And it seems to have continued to be my life's theme. When Daddy wasn't around to answer my "whys" or when he made me scramble for my own, books were my main source of enlightenment, and they have been ever since.

Daddy was Merton M. Smith. Mother was Elizabeth Hardegen Smith, known as Betty or Betz, and my name was Ethel Elizabeth. If I could have been called Elizabeth, Betsy, Betty, or Beth, I believe my entire childhood would have been easier, for I hated the name Ethel Smith. It always sounded to me like a schoolteacher calling me down—harsh and unfriendly. But Mother would not hear of any Elizabeth nicknames, because they were hers, and Ethie, Essel, or Smitty were so horrible that even I did not want them.

While I was in college, Daddy and I made a trip into the Arkansas Ozarks, and as we drove along we started playing hillbilly. I called him "Pappy" and he called me "Susie." When we reached home, we declared our new names to everyone and never allowed any other to be used for us from then on. I started spelling it S-U-S-Y right away, because to me "Susie" Smith sounded like somebody's cook. Years later, I made Susy legal. I thought it would be a good name for the novelist I hoped to be. As it turned out, I went right into parapsychology (or psychical research) instead of novel writing, and the name Ethel Elizabeth Smith, or even Mrs. Ethel Smith-Smith, would have been much more appropriate for a scientific writer.

Both my parents' mothers died young, and neither of them were with their fathers much, and so I never knew any grandparents. My father was a government career man and for a while during the First World War a military officer, and so we traveled a great deal. At no time during my childhood did I ever have any close girl friends. The main thing I can remember about that whole period of my life was being lonely. I always envied those who had large families with whom to enjoy activities and get-togethers—parties and picnics and such. Grandmothers and grandfathers were idealized in my mind; and if I could only have had a big brother or a twin, that would have been heaven for me.

Daddy was commissioned a captain in the Army when I was six, and soon he was transferred back to Washington, D.C. (where I had been born). There we moved into a boardinghouse temporarily, and within just a few days Daddy came down with pneumonia and pleurisy. He was taken in an ambulance to Walter Reed Hospital with a temperature of a hundred and six degrees; and he had been there only a week when Mother caught the flu. An ambulance came for her, and she was put into a room across the hall from Daddy. When they took Mother away, I stood alone on the sidewalk in front of our lodgings and bawled my little heart out.

While convalescing from his near demise, Daddy was sent to Florida for a month's rest. Then Mother came home from the hospital to discover that my throat was acting up very unpleasantly. The condition was at first diagnosed as laryngeal diphtheria, and within three days I was actually at the point of choking to death. In fact, the doctor walked out of the room, leaving Mother alone with me, because, he said, "I can't stand to see the little thing die."

Just then there was a clanking and jingling sound outside, and I indicated curiosity about it. That's me; even when I'm dying, I'm nosy about what's going on outside. Mother looked out the window and saw a 20-Mule Team Borax parade going by. When she held me up to see the big animals as they clomped past with nodding red plumes on their heads and tinkling bells, the lump in my throat seemed to be relieved, and I was able to keep on breathing until the ambulance arrived to take me, too, to Walter Reed Hospital.

This is the first of several miraculous recoveries in my life, and I now give the Lord full credit for them. I used to call such things "chance happenings" or "mere coincidence." I don't any more.

I was just moments away from a tracheotomy all night but was given inhalations of tincture of benzoin—a new process they were trying out on me—and by morning the breath was coming more normally, so the surgery was not necessary. Acute laryngitis was the final diagnosis, and there were soon no further distressful symptoms, except that my voice vanished for a year.

My father was quartermaster at Fort Sill, Oklahoma, during the year I couldn't talk. Because of my illness, Mother and I did not go with him; but later we went on the train to Indianapolis to visit Mother's sisters, and none of us ever did go back to Washington to live. When Daddy joined us, after the war was over, we bought a newly built house a block away from Mother's sister Ivy and moved in. But my globe-trotting father was soon sent to the Philippines, and that is a long, lonely way from Indiana, U.S.A. Mother kept busy at her sewing machine, and I pulled my nose out of books occasionally to play with paper dolls, for which I loved to draw the costumes; but the two of us in a strange town found life very dull.

Fortunately for us, Aunt Ivy brought a friend to meet us, a tiny woman named Nina Sharpe, who was looking for a place to live. When Nina moved into our home to room and board with us, she moved into our hearts as well. She became a second mother to me, and stayed with me all the rest of her life.

Nina was a graduate of the Indianapolis Conservatory of Music, and she played beautiful classical pieces on the piano for us all the time. I took lessons from her for a while, but the simple exercises that had to be practiced endlessly were so tedious that after a few months I gave up. Inspired by Nina, however, my musical education has continued in that I listen avidly to everything from symphonies, operas, concertos, and chamber music to Dixieland jazz. My artistic urges have been taken out instead in writing, drawing, and painting, for all of which I had considerably more patience and aptitude.

A brief résumé of my mental attitudes during my childhood might be necessary here in order to explain the agnosticism I accepted in college. It all goes back to Santa Claus, actually. I believed in him until I was eight years old. He was a living being whom I loved and understood much more than I understood God or Jesus, who didn't even come around at Christmas with a beautiful tree and gifts the way Santa did. When my cousin Margaret in Indianapolis told me there was no Santa Claus, with Mother's reluctant confirmation, it was such a blow that I cried for days. From then on, I don't remember ever believing in anything much.

Neither of my parents had been brought up in churchgoing homes, and whatever religion they might have had did not affect me. I was trained to say my "Now I lay me down to sleep" before retiring, and that is as far as it went. Mother and Daddy never set foot in a church. They both always said, "You can be as good a Christian out of church as in," and since they were ethical people, I believed them. As a token gesture, I was sent to the nearest Sunday school, at first, whenever we moved to a new city; but after finding it difficult to make contact with the unfamiliar children, I stayed home from then on.

In those various Sunday schools—and churches, when I remained for church—I do not recall ever having God presented as a loving Father, or Jesus as anything more than His Son who went around spouting parables about how to live life better. There were Christmas pageants about His birth, and that was nice; but otherwise He was unreal to me. Had I been exposed then to spirit-filled Christians' loving acceptance of Jesus as an active part of their lives, how different my existence would have been! How I envy those who have been raised with the security of a loving Father-God and His Son, Jesus, a shepherd to keep track of them whenever they become lost! As it was, it seems that I was always lost all during my life until recently, with no one to turn to who could find me.

Because I was so bookish, I received taunts in school: "Ethel swallered the dictionary"—a most successful put-down. So I tried to be an exceptionally good sport out of school to make up for it—doing anything I was challenged to do. In winter the boys and I coasted our sleds off high banks or slid them over a frozen pond we discovered behind some big signboards at the end of our street. We played follow the leader, running along the highest scaffoldings on the apartment buildings under construction nearby; we swung like monkeys from ceiling pipes in the basements and jumped from porch roofs into sand piles. Once, I fell when trying to leap across the sidewalk from a high stack of bricks to the top of a shed. I landed on my back on the pavement with a considerable plop but no broken bones, so even that did not stop my career of good sportsmanship . . . then.

The Pacific Ocean seemed to get wider with the passing months, so finally Daddy, by now a major, retired from the Army in order to come home. Then he became affiliated with the Department of Agriculture and was sent to Salt Lake City. Mother put the house up for sale so we could join him, but by the time we finally caught up with him, he was in San Antonio, Texas, a lovely city. The beauty of its semitropical climate, with its palm trees and blooming oleanders, crape myrtle, and queen's crown, enchanted us, and we never lost our love for it.

I became ill soon after we went to San Antonio, and the doctor thought some of my organs had been scrambled by my fall while scampering around on the buildings in Indianapolis. At least, my spleen was topsy-turvy and I was hemorrhaging much of the time. So I was put to bed for a year and had frequent osteopathic treatments to put things back in order.

Of course, I lost all contact with children my own age during this time. All through high school I was a loner who could not relate to my peers, and I *never* had any fun. The caption under my senior-class picture read: "A future artist, a girl with talents in many directions and a likable disposition," but I did not believe a word of it. I knew I was a drip, even if no one else did. And to prove it, I guess, I had a severe case of measles, which started during graduation week, so I missed most of the ceremonies and parties.

During my childhood, I amplified my frustrations by lying

awake at night worrying. In high school, although too shy to talk to the boys I had crushes on, I was quick with a sassy quip around the girls. Then I'd go over every word at night and agonize because it must surely have been the wrong thing to say. And it probably was.

During these lying-awake times, I thought about God a good bit. I can well remember praying and then demanding hotly, "O God, Whoever or Whatever you are, please let me learn the *truth!*"

It was not only during the fretful tossing at night but also whenever we sat out in the yard in the evenings, that I thought about life's eternal questions as we looked at the stars and discussed the vastness of the universe and the relative insignificance of man. Deep in the heart of Texas, the stars really are as big and bright as the song says. At least, they were in my day. Now you have to get far outside a big city before you can really see them. The immensity of the universe was so startling and the questions so overpowering that I was increasingly bewildered. What was especially confusing to me was the fact that everything in life has a definite origin and conclusion, excuse for being, and reasonable explanation—everything, that is, except the greatest and most profound issues of all. If there was a God, Who was He? Where did He come from? How did He originate? How did the universe begin? Would it ever end, and if so, when? I wondered.

Many people ask these questions as I did. It was frightening to be so sure that nowhere was there an answer.

It was during my years at the University of Texas that I was most critical in my thinking—and most divergent from my classmates—because of debating so much with the status quo. Today that is not unusual; many young people do it. Then, my fellow students and roommates just thought me a cantankerous person. Although there were no doubt many radical thinkers on campus, I did not know them or else I might have joined them, for very few of my associates questioned the orthodoxy of their churches or family opinions. I was at odds with everyone most of the time, until I finally stopped arguing . . . with my friends and with myself.

During this time, we had a history teacher who told us, "Man makes God in his own image." My agreement with this was my final push toward becoming an agnostic. H. L. Mencken, the famous atheistic humorist, was my favorite author, especially because he served up his cynicism with a laugh. I've always enjoyed humor, if it is subtle and clever. It has saved me on many occasions.

So, without an organized religion, I developed what seemed to me a philosophy of life that was adequate. I usually behaved myself according to my understanding of the mores of my generation, because it was expedient to do so. But I had brainwashed myself to the point that my slogan was "Always expect the worst so that you won't be disappointed." I was not disappointed, either, for the worst always happened to me. And I thought life was a great big mess.

What most people do when they reach an impasse of this kind in their thinking is just what occurred to me to do. I stopped allowing myself to be involved in conjecture of any kind and managed to keep my mind busy with work, with reading, with studying, and with pleasure. My quest for philosophical truth was completely sidetracked as I reached instead for any and every palliative to replace serious reflection.

For a while, my time was mostly occupied with beaux. I had made the honor role continually in high school but never had any dates. I made up for lost time in college, and my grades revealed it.

Big, tall, dynamic Henry and I became engaged almost immediately after we met, during my third year in college. He was so extra-special I couldn't resist him. Every weekend toward the close of that school year, we talked seriously about running away and getting married; but sanity would prevail when I returned to the dormitory each night and begged my girl friends to talk me out of it. When we put it off once too often, priorities intervened.

Henry had staked out a claim to a gold mine in Colorado the

summer before we met, and we decided we would be married right after school was out and spend the summer working the mine. But when we went to my home in June, I learned that my little Pappy was terminally ill with malignant hypertension —the worst form of high blood pressure. I had not been told how bad he was, because the family had not wanted to worry me, and I had been so immersed in my romance that I hadn't been home for ages.

Daddy was still able to go to his office for a little while each day, but the doctor had forbidden him to drive his car. So he expected me to spend my summer chauffering him back and forth to work.

"But we're getting *married!*" I wailed.

Pappy called me by that nickname he'd been using lately. "I need you, Susy," he said. I stayed, of course. I couldn't let a sick man down.

So Henry spent the summer in Colorado alone, and I worried about him, and also about Daddy, who died in September. I really had not believed in the reality of death. I'd never seen it before, because we had never even been intimate enough with other families to attend funerals. I had no religious belief in a life after death, and so the experience was shattering to me. I began having horrible nightmares every night that we'd buried Daddy and then he came back or that he sat up in his coffin at his funeral and announced that he was still alive. Or even that he'd been buried alive. Frequently I'd jump up screaming, having seen a luminous figure standing beside my bed. All during the fall college term, this went on. My roommate moved out on me, and who was to blame her? For she was awakened most nights by my crying or shrieking in my sleep.

Henry was a law student, so naturally he liked to argue. With my ragged nerves, caused by my frightening dreams, I was very querulous and this made him more aggressive, so we fought much of the time. Finally we decided on a separation, hoping that distance would increase our desire for each other. At mid-term I transferred to the University of Arizona, where I had spent a semester once before; but, unable to concentrate on lessons, I soon gave up and came home. After Henry and I had a big reunion, we began to quarrel once again. So Mother and Nina came to the rescue with an extended vacation tour of the North and East.

Several months later, while we were in Detroit visiting my father's sister Mabel, I heard that my Henry was married. So I moved in with Aunt Mabel, got a job as a secretary in an insurance office, and sent Mother and Nina home without me. Very soon, a cousin introduced me to M. L. (Mo) Smith, and, two months later, still smarting over Henry, I married him on the rebound. But he was not the pleasantest person in the world, as was soon to be discovered, and our marriage was a total foul-up.

Mo and I had been enduring marriage together for a year and a half when we decided to take a vacation in August and drive to Texas. By the time we reached my home in San Antonio, I was desperately ill with a generalized streptococcal septicemia, or blood poisoning, all through my system. Put to bed immediately, I was soon almost comatose with a low-grade fever that kept me lying without stirring or eating for two weeks. Then the infection localized in my left hip, and the pain became so intense that I screamed whenever the joint was moved. Finally life was one long scream to me, even though I tried valiantly to suppress it, and I was taken to the hospital, anesthetized, and put into a plaster cast.

When I regained consciousness, the pain was still intense, and I learned to pray that night. It was the first time I'd ever done any real praying since the feeble efforts of my childhood, and the religious spell did not last past the first few days of my incarceration. But it carried me through—along with the loving prayers of most of the people I knew. When it was all over, I felt rather embarrassed about having weakened in my extremity and prayed, when I still had no real concept of God.

My illness occurred in the days just before the sulfa drugs and penicillin, which are now effective against strep, so the doctor could only give me massive intravenous injections of what he told me was sodium acetylsalicylate (aspirin) and Mercurochrome. Somehow they were effective, and a month or so later all the infection was gone. I was in a cast that started at my waist and went to my ankle on the left side and to my knee on the right side, its purpose being to immobilize that left hip until all the infection was gone. Unknown to me then, it would also stiffen the hip joint so that it wouldn't bend and I would be crippled.

The hospital was so noisy that sleep was impossible, so I was allowed to go home with a practical nurse to take care of me. Mother and Nina also gave me constant attention and set themselves to feeding me well to fatten me up and give me strength. A friend told me when I looked forward with dread to three months in the cast that if I kept each moment occupied, the days and weeks would pass without too much discomfort, and she was right. Holding my arms up in the air over my head, I knitted an afghan, and I even got some reading done— of lightweight books.

Nina, who read aloud beautifully, took me on trips to Tara and Atlanta daily with the newly published *Gone with the Wind*. No one ever loved that book more than I did, reliving every incident as I waited impatiently for each day's chapter. So when Nina had to stop reading, just before the end, I grabbed the book and held it in the air over my head and managed to finish it. Then I cried for hours, for even then Clark Gable was Rhett Butler in my mind, and I hated Scarlett for not appreciating him as I would have.

While my days were endurable, the nights were wearying as I lay in my plaster straitjacket. When I was safely convalescing, a friend who had been at my home when I was first taken to the hospital told me that the doctor had said I'd had one chance in a thousand to pull through. The knowledge of the recent imminence of my death stayed in my mind constantly after this, particularly at night. No matter what time I dropped off to sleep initially, for years I awoke on the dot of midnight shaking with terror about dying.

Mo had stayed in Texas to be with me during my illness, but he was never home before three in the morning. Once awakening at midnight, I was never able to get back to sleep until his return, and I'd lie and worry until his car pulled up and his key sounded in the lock. What I thought about was invariably the question of life and death. Where would I be now if I had died? Extinct, I thought, without having given life even half a try. I was definitely not ready to die. Why, I had hardly lived yet, certainly not any of the happy times one has a right to expect from life. With nothing more than a harrowed childhood and a miserable marriage to show for it, what had it been worth to have lived at all? I wanted to give to the world, to make my life worth something to my fellow men. At that time I hoped to have children and at least make my existence count for that, for I thought they were my only hope of immortality. To have my life end then would have been some terrible caustic joke by a hateful, avenging God. Surely, if He existed at all, He couldn't be that mean.

An agnostic does not face death easily.

CHAPTER III

"...Either to Tell, or to Hear Some New Thing"*

By 1955, when my psychical research began, I had become a sophisticated, modern woman who had done a lot of living but had acquired very little spiritual growth. After two and a half years of desolate marriage, I'd obtained a divorce, then had an operation to restore motion to my left hip. This left me with a limp, because one leg was a couple of inches shorter than the other, so I walked with a cane.

Possibly my most rewarding experience during this entire period was when I sang for several years in a church choir. In 1940, Mother sold our Cape Cod cottage in San Antonio, and we moved to Oakland, Maryland, where she had just inherited her old family home. This was my first experience living in a small town, and it was, on the whole, most enjoyable. The thing that was especially strange for me was going to church, but since that was the center of activity, Mother, Nina, and I soon found ourselves busy with Sunday-school classes and the Women's Society, covered-dish suppers, rummage sales, etc.; and I even added my untrained second soprano to the otherwise excellent choir.

Yet as I sat through the church services, my mind argued with much that went on. I would not repeat the Apostles'

* Acts 17:21 (King James)

Creed, for to me it was not believable, and much that was said made my stomach tie up in knots of rebellion. When I asked to join the church—to give me a legitimate excuse to sing in the choir—the minister would not let me because of my divorce; but after a while he was transferred and his replacement greeted me kindly and invited me in from the cold. It was a traditional Methodist church, however, and, although its members were warm and friendly, it did nothing to change my arbitrary point of view, which was still negative and still seeking in all the wrong ways.

My illness and operations had kept me from ever practicing the journalism I'd majored in at college, but in Oakland I had the opportunity to work on a small-town newspaper. I discovered that, with my gregarious nature, newspaper work was what I had obviously been designed for, and my "Shopping with Susy" column became a pet with advertisers. So when Mother died, in 1949, I hied myself to Florida and started putting out a *Shopping with Susy* tabloid-size shopping guide in Daytona Beach. I also bought a miniature dachshund puppy (red, to match my hair) and it was the best move of my life. Junior was to be my constant companion and solace for my loneliness for twelve years.

One of the nice things that happened to me in Florida was meeting Margaret Sanders Adams (now Mrs. David Huenergardt), the daughter of Colonel Harlan Sanders, who was later to become famous, and wealthy, as the colossus of Kentucky Fried Chicken. By the fall of 1954 I was looking for a nice, dry climate for the arthritis with which my strep infection had left me, and Margaret was in Salt Lake City, bombarding me with letters about the wonderful conditions there. So Nina, Junior, and I set out to join her.

As we drove along through Mormon country, we felt like pioneers ourselves as we traversed the vast, bare reaches of Nebraska and southern Wyoming and then Utah's golden, aspenglowing mountains. When we came out onto the promontory marked "This Is the Place," we stopped and looked with hushed anticipation across the magnificent valley, a desert when the Mormons first saw it but now blooming with beautiful flowers and plants because of their efforts. We were as sure as they that we had achieved Utopia at last.

As we journeyed along, we saw many house trailers on the highway, and they looked very good to me. It seemed that those who traveled as much as we did would have a lot easier time if they did not have to be packing and unpacking a car constantly. With that attitude, it is not surprising that it was impossible to find an apartment to suit us; but almost the first trailer we looked at answered all our requirements. It was towed to a trailer park not far from downtown, and with the help of Margaret and her twelve-year-old son, Trigg, we moved right in.

After our nine-room home in Maryland, living in the Gingerbread House, as we named our new acquisition, seemed like living in a pencil box. Still, it had a bedroom with a double bed, a bathroom with a shower, and a convertible bed in the cozy living room for Nina. We soon found room in its many closets and cupboards for all our possessions, and then we began to realize there was room for us as well.

I immediately acquired a job with the Newspaper Agency Corporation, which handled the advertising for both the Salt Lake City *Tribune* and the *Deseret News and Telegram*, and was put to writing neighborhood shopping columns, which appeared in both daily papers. Soon I was also doing a "Shopping with Susy" page in the *Sunday Tribune Magazine* section, with numerous pictures taken with a Polaroid camera while visiting the various stores.

Nina and Junior went with me frequently when making my rounds to the neighboring communities for advertising copy. Maggie and Trigg lived nearby, and we saw them often. And we made a new friend in Veryl Smith, who, as Mrs. Karl Romer, now lives near me in Tucson and is a very close friend.

So now we have the setting and the cast of characters for the new drama that is about to unfold. For here is where psychical research discovered me and got me into a hotbed of interest . . . and trouble.

Much as I do not advise it for others, it must be admitted that my start in the psychic field came through the use of the Ouija board. Actually, what instigated my interest was a book called *The Unobstructed Universe*, by Stewart Edward White. I saw it on the bookshelf of an acquaintance and recalled that we'd had it at home. A friend had sent it to us, but none of us had ever read it and it was donated to the library along with most of our other books when we left Oakland.

I asked about it, and its owner said, "I haven't read it either, but I think it attempts to prove that there is life after death." I somehow had a compulsion to know what was in that book, so I borrowed it. Nina and Veryl Smith were also interested, and we read it aloud together.

Now, *The Unobstructed Universe* purports to be a true account, and a man with the solid reputation of Stewart Edward White could hardly have written lies in the name of truth. He already had a big following as an author of travel and adventure books at the time he turned to writing in the psychic field. Yet, since the subject matter is the messages obtained from White's deceased wife, Betty, through a non-professional medium, naturally we were inclined to wonder about it. The evidence he gave seemed so strong, however, that it aroused my interest in conditions in the spirit world after death, as described by Betty. After we finished that book, we got another of White's at the library: *With Folded Wings*. In it we read that our loved ones who have passed on would like to communicate with us to reassure us there is really no death and that they are often with us. White suggested that we make the first move toward contact and they would co-operate.

The chance that this might be true, that my parents might still be alive somewhere in "the great beyond," was enthralling to me, even though I was highly skeptical at the same time. There had been only one previous incident that had caused me to consider the possibility that Mother was sending me a message, and I had eventually dismissed it. For, the Christmas before she died, Mother had given me a musical powder box that played "Oh! Susanna." But, every time I raised the lid and the tinkly tune began, it upset me, for I knew by then she was dying, and hearing the music for the words "Oh! Susanna, don't you cry for me" always reminded me of the fact. Mother was satisfied that she'd had a fulfilled life, and she was not afraid to die. But I did not believe in life after death and could not face losing her forever. Nina and I gave her devoted care, and for the first time in my life I was able to do things for her in return for the love she had always showered on me.

She waited until spring, 1949, to leave us, just two months before her sixtieth birthday; and the night she passed on, she said all the most perfect things to make us feel as peaceful as possible about it because we realized she was comfortable with the idea of dying. She reiterated her love for us and her appreciation for the care we had given her, and then she went away.

I would never play my music box, because it brought tears to my eyes. It sat neglected on my dresser until four o'clock one morning a little over a month after Mother's death. Then it began to play of its own accord. I awoke with a start, somehow comforted by the strains of "Oh! Susanna, don't you cry for me," for the message seemed to come straight from Mother. But my rational mind immediately turned off such thoughts and I tried to find the logical explanation for the box's playing when no one had touched it. I couldn't. There was no way to figure how the lid had become jarred loose; we did not have mice; there were no vibrations in the house. I could not allow myself to think of the incident as in any way supernormal, but, all the same, there was a little feeling of hope that Mother might possibly be taking this means to tell me she was still around somewhere and still caring.

This incident came to my mind as I read White's book, and I questioned if it had any significance. Still wondering about it, I put the book down and took Junior for a walk. We crossed a large field, and right in the middle of it I was suddenly infused with a warm, loving awareness of Mother's presence. She was so close to me that I could have reached out and hugged her. I *knew* it was Mother and no one could ever tell me it was not. There had never been any feeling of her presence in all the six years since her death, until my mind was opened to the possibility of her still being alive, so this was a beautifully tender confirmation. I went back into the house determined to make the attempt to communicate with her to see if there might be some way she could prove life after death to me.

While writing this book, I was pleased to find, in the September 7, 1976, issue of the *National Enquirer* that evangelist Billy Graham, in an exclusive interview, had revealed the experience that gave him proof of life after death. The Reverend Dr. Graham said, "I was sitting at the bedside of my maternal grandmother as she lay dying of old age. The room was dark, but suddenly it filled with light!" The window shades were drawn and the light was switched off—yet the room was lit up, he said. Just then, his grandmother sat up in bed, something she had not been able to do for days, and her pale face flushed with color. She smiled and cried, "I see Jesus! He has His arms outstretched toward me."

"Then," says the evangelist, "she uttered the name of her husband, Ben, who had died several years earlier, after losing an arm and eye in the Civil War.

"'I see Ben!' she said, her face beaming with life. 'He's whole again. His arm and eye have returned. . . . I'm coming, Ben!' With those words my grandmother slumped over and died—and the room returned to darkness."

We used the Ouija avidly all during the spring of 1955, and it was my mother who purported to talk with me. Then, one day, the board wrote, "Get a pencil," and so I started doing what is called automatic writing. This continued for some months, and it eventually got so that the messages would come on the typewriter as well as by pencil. During this time, Mother was able to convince me that it was really she who was communicating. This was partly because she lectured me just as much as she had while in her physical body on earth. Now she continually gave me dissertations on such topics as "love" and "development of character" and "positive thinking." I could have read the same stuff in the *Reader's Digest* with much less trouble, so found these lessons a bit wearying. Yet, by dint of sheer repetition, she gradually made the point that I must personally make an effort to improve myself in the areas she was insisting upon.

"Love is the most important thing and you need to love all the time," she wrote. "You must learn to think more kindly of others. You are much too critical. You need to love everyone, not just those to whom you are attached and who are kind to you. It takes real effort to love everyone, but you can do it. And then everything will go smoothly and your life will be a big success while you are on earth as well as afterwards. Heaven is the state of love."

I began to make a special effort to follow her advice; and when results became obvious in my life, I was glad she had been so persistent.

Another thing Mother wrote to me about was God; and I, who had been an agnostic most of my life, began finally to realize that there is a God in Heaven Who is a Loving Father Who would take care of me if I would only turn to Him. It was a very gradual process for me to start to include God in my thinking, but I did give it a try as time went on. I still did not pray to Him, however, until the period, just about a year later, when the "voices" tried to take over my mind.

Mother had even warned me in advance about those, but I had not really paid attention to her. She said that bad spirits could influence those on earth who tried to communicate and thus made themselves receptive to them. She wanted me to be wary of them at all times. She told me that those who had died with hatred in their hearts had to be converted to good, and this was a long, hard process on their part and on that of the ministering angels who tried to work with them to improve their evil natures.

She said that she was my guardian angel, explaining that those who love us when they die continue to love us, and they try to help us when they can. When we finally learned to use the typewriter together, she wrote many pages about all this. They were eventually published as "Mother's Chapter," in *Confessions of a Psychic*. But while I was still in Salt Lake

City, I was beginning to get only the faintest glimmerings of what she meant about any of it.

One night, toward the end of April of that year, when Veryl and I were using the Ouija board, something peculiar occurred. The word Kizzie was spelled out, and that was Nina's mother's name. Kizzie wrote that she came to tell us that Nina would not live long. Although Nina was seventy-two years old then, we had no idea she was in ill health; but, on Memorial Day, just about a month later, she dropped dead of a heart attack.

CHAPTER IV

"I Am Watching over Them..."*

My friend Fay Peters, on reading an early draft of the manuscript of this book, said that even though I had been denying God for over half my life, she had seen a definite pattern emerge. It is obvious to her that the Lord has been protecting me and leading me throughout my life to the point that I was ready for action when He reached out and grabbed me to become a Christian.

Looked at in that light, it is now obvious to me also that I have had His care all the time without being aware of it. Certainly the 20-Mule Team Borax parade coming by at the very moment when the doctor had affirmed that I was choking to death seems more than coincidence. And it was almost miraculous that, in the days before sulfa and penicillin, I came through a streptococcal blood poisoning with nothing worse than a limp. Just a few years before, President Coolidge's son Calvin had died of the same kind of septicemia. The sixteen-year-old boy got a blister on the top of his right toe while playing tennis in sneakers without wearing socks. Soon his entire leg was streaked with blood poisoning, and then he was gone. Something saved me from the same fate.

It is clear to me now that the Lord was also with me all the time in my psychical research. Had there not been a great deal of protection, I could very well have gone completely dotty

* Jer. 44:27 (New American Bible)

over the voices when they began talking in my mind. My late friend Clarissa Mulders always nagged at me for my rigidity, since after the trouble the Ouija board got me into (it led eventually to the voices in my mind), I continually warned everyone else away from it. She would say, "Susy, why do you insist that I must not try to use Ouija? Give me the privilege to make mistakes if I want to. I'd rather take my own chances of getting into trouble, even if the same thing might happen to me that happened to you."

As an analogy, if you see someone else, especially someone you love, starting to jump into a vat of boiling water in which you have just been almost scalded, you can't help but warn her against it. It could be true that many persons have been in that same vat under different circumstances and merely had a pleasantly warm bath. Still, the fact that on numerous, unpredictable occasions the thermostat was out of control and the water so hot as to be dangerous should cause people to avoid it altogether. At least, that's the way it seems to me, and that's why I am so adamant about not making any effort at spirit communication. Many in the psychic field are irritated by my insistence on this, but it has become a major theme with me.

(The day this was written, I had lunch with a lady who was just over a nervous breakdown. It had come about because a Ouija board told her the man she loved had just been killed and she'd had no way to check the truth of the statement for several days. When she learned that he was not dead, she had already collapsed from anguish and uncertainty and was in the hospital.)

The fact that I did not break down similarly during my efforts to communicate convinces me that I was protected. I have also had many experiences while driving that reveal a watchful eye by someone who had my interest at heart, especially when I was doing my soloing about the country. Once, about 1953, when sprinting west on a deserted stretch of level highway in New Mexico, I let the car out to eighty-five miles an hour for a while. Suddenly I seemed to smell a whiff of burning rubber. I immediately slowed down, only moments before there was a blowout of the left rear tire. A passerby changed it for me, and that was that. Except that as I proceeded along on my trip—pretty well shaken by my narrow escape and addicted from thence forward to greatly reduced speeds—I mulled over and over in my mind the narrow escape I'd had. I kept wondering, and an still wondering, how it could be possible for an odor of burning rubber from a rear tire to travel forward. The tire was behind me, and any fumes should naturally have been retreating, shouldn't they? How could they have reached my nose up front in a closed car? And anyway, would a tire having a sudden blowout give advance warning with a smell of burning rubber?

There seems to be considerable indication of supernormal protection during my travels in the spring and fall of 1955. By late June, after Nina's death, Margaret and I were ready to move to California to seek our fortunes. During the month, room had been made in the Gingerbread House for Margaret and Trigg, their parakeet, and their many possessions, but we found it to be a tight squeeze. After we got out on the highway with the trailer in tow, it was discovered that something was wrong with my little Chevrolet Bel Air, and pulling such a load was too much for it. We eventually managed to arrive in Las Vegas, where a defective gasket was repaired, and then all was well; but in the meantime we had a few rough times as we tried to shinny up the mountains with our heavy load.

Between St. George, Utah, and Glendale, Nevada, there are eighty-three miles of straight, uninhabited desert. There was nothing in Glendale but a service station and a restaurant. And there was little else between it and Las Vegas but fifty miles of expanse. But in Glendale we had one of those little miracles that made me suspect Mother had really meant it when she said she was my guardian angel. Perhaps, I might now say, it was some other angels or Jesus keeping an eye on us; but whoever it was, we were most grateful when we pulled into the garage at Glendale at 8:30 P.M. and discovered the trailer had just had a flat. Not out in any of the eighty-three desolate miles behind us, or the fifty ahead of us, but right where there was a service station so that it could be repaired and we could continue on our journey.

Being still an agnostic and a very critical observer, I had many questions about the things that began to happen in my life. But also being a newspaper reporter by trade, I knew enough to start writing the details down; and so I had what practically amounted to a diary to confirm my memory when I started writing *Confessions of a Psychic* and now this book. I will mention only the most outstanding ones here, but there were numerous small helpful events that had a miraculous quality about them.

I couldn't find any kind of job in California that suited me and so spent all my spare time reading books on psychic phenomena, which I found in the library. There I discovered the works of Dr. J. B. Rhine, then of the Parapsychology Laboratory at Duke University, and came to realize that there is scientific research going on in the psychic field. I presumed from this that Dr. Rhine's laboratory would be the headquarters for research about life after death, but it was not. I was to learn that it is a common misconception that Dr. Rhine is interested in trying to prove survival, because he usually suggests in his books that his research in telepathy, clairvoyance, and precognition (prophecy) would tend to indicate that man does have a soul, which inevitably leads to the possibility that it might survive death. On page 217 of *The Reach of the Mind* he says: "Any sort of survival of any portion of the personality, for any length of time, holds such significance for human thinking and feeling as to dwarf almost all other scientific discovery by comparison." These were my sentiments exactly!

I wrote to Dr. Rhine, and an associate answered with information that prepared me with the idea of going to Durham and observing, in the hope that perhaps eventually I could acquire some kind of grant for research work. Of course, going there meant trundling the Gingerbread House across the entire country. The small bequest I had received from Nina was not going to last forever, so I could not spend the money to have my home on wheels pulled by a truck. I had to do it myself (with the help of my car and, of course, with Junior's moral support). Maggie and Trigg were already back East by then.

All my neighbors in the mobile-home court where I was living squeaked and squealed in protest. One man frankly told me, "I wouldn't even try to pull a trailer that far alone myself, and I don't have the handicap you do." I agreed with him, but what else could I do? By then, I had begun to have an opinion that has carried me through some pretty trying situations since then: "I can do anything I have to do." Now, of course, the statement is amended to read: "With God's help, I can do anything I have to do."

On this cross-country junket with the trailer in tow, there were at least three distinct incidents that revealed the caring assistance I was having. The first spectacular one occurred just outside Ozona, in the hills of West Texas.

There was a heavy fog at first, as we drove from the town, and then the sunshine peered through it and began to glare in my eyes. About nine o'clock, as we picked up some speed over the hills, persistent impressions started bombarding me to pull over to the side of the road and stop.

"Better get my sunglasses out of the glove compartment," I thought, but they could not be reached while driving, so I decided to wait until the next roadside park to stop for them. There is a hand brake to manipulate in order to slow a trailer, you know, as well as the controls of the car; and it would be a bit complicated to pull into the gravel alongside the road.

Then I thought that my eyes were not really opened up yet that morning. "Better get out some eye drops." But they, too, were in the glove compartment. Right on top of this came the idea that it would be smart to stop to see if the gas tanks on the front of the trailer were holding securely with a new bolt that had been put on. These impressions were all so insistent that, silly as it seemed to me to stop right along the highway where there was no pullout, I finally did.

The Gingerbread House bumped to an unusually jerky halt, and I reflected on the dangers of pulling over onto roadside gravel, determining never to do it again. I got out my eye drops and used them, and put on the dark glasses; then I decided, "Well, all right, let's just look at those tanks. Maybe there is some reason for pulling over."

I found the tanks okay, but the connection that plugged the trailer brake into the car's electric outlet had become un-hitched. The socket was dragging on the ground! If I'd tried to go down a steep hill, or even to stop suddenly, that trailer would have wrapped itself around my neck.

"Thank you, guardian angels," I said, with more belief in their reality than ever before.

I routed my entourage by way of San Antonio in order to spend Christmas with old friends; and then, becoming eager to get to Durham and begin my survival research, I resumed the tour on January 9. Just outside of San Antonio, on Loop 13, suddenly a car pulled out onto the highway not more than twenty-five feet in front of us. I immediately jammed on the foot brake of the car and pulled the trailer hand brake with such force that everything went out of control.

"Help me, help me!" I cried. And help was there. Although the car and the trailer buckled back and forth and turned themselves completely around, nothing overturned, and we didn't crash into the car in front that had caused the trouble. Junior had been thrown from the seat to the floor, but, thank-fully, was not damaged in any way. The Bel Air was revealed on inspection to have a blown-out tire, and there was a clanking noise in the trailer wheel, but that was all. Passing men, who stopped to help, assured the police it had not been my fault, changed my tire, and suggested I drive along until a garage could be found with a mechanic on duty to take care of the trailer problem. So off we went once again, unnerved but not disabled.

Soon the trailer tire was completely shot, and I pulled over alongside the Austin Highway. Then something else occurred that indicated the beautiful assistance available to me. A young man named John stopped to offer his help and then gave us his entire day. First he rented an automatic jack from the closest service station and took the wheel off. In the wreck the drum had become almost unriveted from the rim, and a rivet had dropped down inside and ripped the tire to pieces.

So John took Junior and me and the wheel in his car back to San Antonio, where, while the wheel was being welded, he bought my lunch and told me his life story in a charming Texas accent. He even got me a new tire wholesale! When the wheel was repaired, late in the afternoon, we returned and he put it on for me. Do you think for one minute that God did not send this man in my time of need? I know He did.

The last near escape on that trip occurred as I was approaching Durham, too thoroughly exhausted to care what happened to us. I had been making a push to get to my destination that night, driving for hours on what were called limited access highways that went all over North Carolina. They were straight highways set below the surface of the ground so that you felt you were driving in a ditch or canyon all the time, and there was not an inch to spare alongside the road to pull over on if necessary. Occasionally an EXIT sign would suggest that somewhere off in one direction or another there was a town, but nothing was ever mentioned about whether or not gasoline was available. And the Chevy needed gasoline desperately.

As the needle hovered at the EMPTY mark and the clock said it was close to midnight, I began to mutter to myself and to my guardian angels about our plight. Finally, in desperation, I turned off at an exit to try to find gasoline, but after some miles driving on a narrow country road through the hovering pine trees, all that was revealed was a small, tightly closed, sound-asleep village without a single filling station to its name. There was nothing else to do but reverse our tracks and return to the highway.

The only place to turn was a big, muddy field where excavations had been going on; and in the middle of the turn I realized that deep trenches had been dug all around it. In the slippery ooze the car and the trailer skidded nearer and nearer the edge. Almost collapsing with fatigue by then, I honestly did not care! When I had to make a maneuver that took the trailer so close to the cliff I was sure its wheels were within inches of going over, instead of stopping and getting out into the mud and estimating how much space I had, I just pulled on around. "To hell with it," I said. "If we go over, we go over." We almost did.

Back on the highway, it was another bunch of miles until we arrived on the outskirts of Durham, and the car eagerly lapped up the first gasoline we came to. And so to bed as soon as we found a place to stop, with a few exhausted thanks to my guardian angels and bright hopes for the morrow, when I would visit the Parapsychology Laboratory for the first time. But not one word of appreciation to the Lord, who did it all.

CHAPTER V

"...Distress and Anguish Have Come upon Me"*

After being graciously received at the Parapsychology Laboratory, I immediately spoke of my desire to enter into research designed to prove life after death. From then on, I seemed to be left alone by almost everyone and eventually learned why: "survival research" was a dirty word there. Nothing concerning it was going on; and the only work in which I would be able to participate involved itemizations of successes and failures in telepathy and clairvoyance tests. This required the use of figures, which have always done me in. So, instead, my effort was expended at home every night trying to improve my automatic writing with Mother in the event that it might bring some evidence that would convince the laboratory people, and ultimately *me*, of the reality of life after death. But when I tried to work up really inspiring conversations with Mother, it always seemed impossible to get a good contact. I was hardly aware of it then, but already the spirit intruders were bothering me.

Seeing that I was getting nowhere fast, and practically having to bite bullets every night in order to survive the pain inflicted on my body by the damp, rainy, and snowy weather, after seven weeks it seemed expedient to leave Durham. I wanted to go somewhere that was warm; and after being so

* Psalm 119:143 (New American Bible)

long alone, it would also be nice if it were a place with old friends. So the Gingerbread House and Junior and his mama took off for Daytona Beach, where *Shopping with Susy* had once provided entertainment and friendship for us.

The main thing I had learned at the Parapsychology Lab was to be critical and objective. If I must continue my attempts at survival research, which no one there condoned, it should be done with strict objectivity. My reading should consist of only "critical" books—which gave no philosophy about life after death and carried no "message." I have always been tremendously grateful for this counsel, because it allowed me to maintain a certain balance when I soon got into so much trouble—by *not* following it.

In Daytona Beach, where I settled down to a peaceful existence in a palm-tree-shaded mobile-home park, Mother and I began doing a great deal of automatic writing on the typewriter, our channels now being clear . . . for about three months. Then all hell broke loose!

It is not easy for me to write about what occurred next, for it is obvious that many readers will decide I had a psychotic episode. And yet those who have written to me sharing similar occurrences and thanking me for exposing my own to the light of public scrutiny in *Confessions of a Psychic* have convinced me that it is to good purpose to be frank about this. If my experience will frighten anybody away from attempting to communicate with spirits when he does not know anything about how to control the situation, then it is worth recording. So stay with me as a very tender area of my life is laid bare.

For the record, it must be admitted that when my mind was besieged by the bad guys, I was still as sane and normal as ever before. My mental state would have been the same on any day of my life if I had been plagued by any external menace. Here is a good example: There are some young rascals in Tucson who delight in making obscene phone calls. These are not the filthily depraved calls one receives in New York City, which seems to be a hell house of evil-minded phone perverts. But the Tucson boys are still quite obnoxious. One evening when I answered my phone, a voice said, "Do you want to go to bed?" I hung up on him immediately. He or one of his chums called later and said, "Won't you please talk to me?" I replied, "No, and I've called the sheriff about you," and hung up again. He knew the sheriff wouldn't be able to locate him, and I'd apparently made him mad, so he called back nine times during that weekend. I answered at first, but then, realizing it was a siege, stopped altogether. Once, during the middle of the night, he let the phone ring thirty-five times before he gave up. Now, all this was very annoying and I was naturally distressed. But I was not mentally disturbed by it. This is the same way it was when the voices tried to take over in my mind.

Attempting to develop my own mediumship without instruction, which is exactly what I was doing without even knowing it, I began to go through various experiences that a trained medium could control but that I could not. Getting into the clairsentient phase without being aware of it, suddenly I began hearing voices in my mind. Just as I awoke on the morning of June 2, singing in my head were the words, "Happy birthday to you, happy birthday to you." I realized it was Mother and thanked her, but somehow this did not cause me to recognize that a new phase of my psychic development had started.

It was my Aunt Ivy who spoke to me next, several days later. The words were said in my mind in an area completely separate from the place where my own thoughts were being produced. There were no voice tones to be recognized, just the words, "Aunt Ivy is talking to you, Susy Ethel." Since the Ethel had long been dismissed from my life and from my thoughts, this was a bit evidential to me, for Aunt Ivy had died shortly after I started calling myself Susy and had never learned to make the transition from Ethel.

She went on, "I was sure you were ready to try to communicate with us in this manner. I am beaming these words into your mind telepathically, and you understand them." She then began to tell me to try to reach her children and convince them of life after death. While she was talking, the words came, "Let me try it, let me try it," and then Mother took over the conversation. After that, for several days we talked back and forth a lot. And it was definitely Mother, because she even began to boss me just as she used to do: "Don't put that egg there, you'll knock it off"; things like that.

Very soon, however, the mischief-makers tried to get into the act. And they frightened me nearly to death before they were through with it. When all kinds of absurd words began to be spoken in my mind, obviously not from anyone who had a right to talk to me, I panicked at first.

"I must be going crazy," I thought. They replied, "Yes, you are going crazy. You're definitely losing your mind. We'll drive you crazy." They took up this as a refrain and said it in my mind all day long: "Susy's going crazy. Susy's going crazy."

I tried to give myself some kind of a fight talk. "You're not a sissy, Susy. You have never found anything in life yet that you can't overcome, and you'll lick this."

The intruders latched onto that: "Susy's a sissy, Susy's a sissy." But they also continued with, "You're going crazy. We will drive you crazy."

I thought some juvenile delinquents must be after me, for they were really being very silly. But when this kind of silliness is going on inside of your own mind, then you might as well face up to it: you've got problems.

The first thing I thought to do was to visit a medium for advice, and she told me that many people were invaded by spirit intruders when they tried communicating on their own without knowing how to control the situation. She did not seem in the least worried about me; and she had only two, rather odd, suggestions for removing my internal enemies: First she told me to dip my hands and arms up to the elbows in water and then fling the water from them. This would also fling out the intruding entities, she declared. Her other idea was only slightly more sensible: I should go outside and stand barefoot with my back against a tree, to gain strength from it. Somehow I doubted that either of these was going to succeed in routing my dangerous antagonists. Certainly my flinging water from my elbows brought only laughter from them. All during the first night, however, when I had trouble sleeping because of the constant talk in my mind, I kept going outside and walking up and down. Then I would step out of my slippers and lean my back against the big palm tree in front of the Gingerbread House . . . rather squeamishly, I must admit, because palms are famous for harboring those big roach-like insects known in Florida as palmetto bugs.

It was not until the sky began to hint that the reassurance of daylight was approaching that I got to sleep. And the second day of my siege was even worse. By nighttime I was thoroughly alarmed. I called out to everyone I knew in the spirit world: Mother, Daddy, Aunt Ivy, Nina, my grandparents. "Help me," I cried. "Get me some help, please!" Trying to sleep and being unable to have a moment's peace because of the insistent chatter, I got up and started reading a detective story. This got my mind on something else, fortunately, so that I couldn't hear the voices. But when I became too drowsy to read and tried bed again, there they were.

It is hard to understand why it didn't occur to me right away to try to convert these intruders. If I had read "Mother's Chapter" aloud to them, with all it gave about how earthbound spirits must learn to progress and work to improve themselves, perhaps it would have helped. I probably was too frightened, or too involved with them to be able to stand back and think about the situation.

You see, I didn't know what these things were that were talking in my mind. All I had read and previously experienced made me think they were the spirits of evil men, but I was not sure about that. Even though I maintained non-belief in such things, I couldn't be confident they were not devils or demons or elementals, and I didn't know what they might do to me. My reading had revealed poltergeist cases where such unknown entities had inflicted bodily damage as well as mental, and they had even killed persons on occasion.

Perhaps no one but God could counteract their power; and so I finally prayed to Him a strong prayer for assistance. It seemed unlikely that He might be paying any kind of personal attention to me, but it was worth giving Him a try, I reasoned. So, standing tall in the middle of the trailer, I said firmly to the invisible intruders, "There is a power greater than any of you and I know how to reach it." And then, tentatively at first, and then with more and more emphasis and vigor, I prayed.

"Dear Lord," I cried, "I don't know Who you are or What you are. I only know there is some Great Force that rules this universe. It is to You that I pray now for help. I am desperate. If this keeps on much longer I know I'll lose my sanity. Please, dear God, if You are there, come to my aid in a hurry. Get these voices out of my mind. Please. . . ."

In just a few moments a voice spoke in my mind in gentler language than previously. With a kindly attitude it said, "Your rescuer has arrived. I have come from a far place to help you. There will be no more trouble." He convinced me, and I slipped back into bed as if into my new friend's sheltering arms.

"Thank you, God, for sending help," I said, relaxed and ready for sleep.

The new voice continued to lull me: "There now, rest. You're safe. Just relax. Come to me, I can protect you." I reached out toward him yearningly in my thoughts. But he continued, "Come to me now. Leave your body . . . slip right out of your body and come to me."

That really hit my panic button. I started up quickly, a cold, hard lump in the middle of my stomach, terrified because I knew he was evil, after all. By then I had read enough about out-of-body experiences to know how dangerous they are. People who could do such things as astral projection, as this experience is also called, learned to realize that if their consciousnesses were away from their bodies too long or under negative circumstances, a spirit malefactor could move right in and possess them.

"You're evil!" I shouted, jumping from my bed as if it might be possible to run away from him. He laughed and laughed.

"I almost had you," he exulted. "One more minute and

you'd have come soaring right out to me. Then you'd never have been able to get back into your body."

I had a bad case of the shakes. "Go away, please," I cried, and then appealed again to Mother, Daddy, God, anybody.

"Oh, I'll get you, never fear," he said. "I'll either kill you or drive you insane. You'll never publish that book."

I went back to my detective story and read until I was so exhausted that I dropped off to sleep the minute my head touched the pillow.

Next morning, as soon as I awoke, he was there, trying to kill me, exactly as he had promised. He was constantly sending some kind of electric shocks through my body. They were not nervous shocks or anything like an evidence of tension, although of course that was my first explanation for them. They were different and worse, completely debilitating and shattering, and they weakened my whole system.

He was also by now beginning the profanity bit—talking to me in the dirtiest words he could say. This was before the era when one found vulgar four-letter words in almost any reading matter; I was completely unused to them and they revolted me. But my discomfiture only made him continue with it all the more.

I had not at that time learned that this technique of using profanity is standard operating procedure during this type of spirit obsession. To my knowledge, the physical shocks to my system are relatively unusual, but many other revolting things have occurred to various people who have dabbled with communication. One of these is sending filthy sexual imagery into the mind and instilling sexual urges. Fortunately, I was spared that.

As he endeavored either to kill me with his shocks of etheric lightning or else to bore me to death with his lurid language, I suddenly discovered how to finish off my antagonist. (Undoubtedly this was God's way of answering my prayer.) Once, the intruding creep tried to use a dirty phrase unknown to me —my knowledge of profanity was not broad—and he couldn't get it into my mind. Realizing how I was innocently blocking him, I laughed. Then I taunted him: "You aren't so much, after all. You can't say anything I don't know." I really thought that was funny and had a good laugh at him.

Then the aggressor did not find it a fight any more. He hated to be laughed at, and he degenerated in his own eyes, as well as mine, from a bold adventurer, playing with this woman's mind, to a sulky, invisible derelict. He particularly did not understand the fact that I could enjoy myself, even at his expense.

"How can you laugh at me?" he asked. "If I were in your position, I would hate me. I have really been trying to kill you." He could understand hate, but not humor, apparently. My lack of rancor toward him after all his evil intent was incomprehensible to him.

"You don't hate," he said. "I can see into your mind and read your thoughts, and I don't see hatred for anyone, even me. I don't understand you."

This encouraged me no end. Evidently Mother's efforts at my improvement had shown results, after all.

"I've spent the past year trying to learn to love my fellow men," I told him. And that, of course, reminded me of "Mother's Chapter," and I read it aloud to him immediately. He apparently listened. When it was finished, he said, "So that's why these hazy-looking folks around me are always insisting they can see beautiful things I can't see and hear beautiful music and all that." He thanked me for giving him this information, and then my mind was quiet and no one talked in it all day. The next morning, it was apparently some other individual who intruded himself upon me with his "I'm going to kill you!"

"Oh, no you won't," I replied. "I'm going to convert you instead." And apparently he was converted, for after he heard "Mother's Chapter," he, too, disappeared. There were a succession of such intrusions all during that summer, but I learned to control them by reading aloud at least once every day, and spending most of the rest of my time concentrating on books that held my interest.

I realized that it was only intelligent to stop all efforts to communicate with Mother. When this was done, and my mind was kept constantly occupied with other things, there was no trouble from the spooks. Then, in early December, another concerted effort to wreck me became apparent. Well, perhaps my first physical damage was not due to evil entities trying to hurt me, but certainly the subsequent events can be blamed only on them. On December 4, I was in the yard with Junior, who was romping with a puppy a neighbor boy had just bought. The pup got himself tangled in my feet and tripped me. I threw myself to keep from stepping on him and landed solidly on the ground with my right arm against a brick bordering the flower bed. The crrrrrrack sounded loud and clear as my wrist broke in two places.

I was able to endure the pain enough to get myself to a clinic, where the arm was put in a cast; then I lived in a fairly satisfactory manner for the several months until it was removed. But it wasn't the easiest thing I'd ever done. My biggest problem was exercising Junior, because my right arm was my walking arm. When the cane was not used, I hobbled uncomfortably. But my pet was used to his daily hikes around the neighborhood, and was most insistent.

The arm was out of the cast in ten weeks, numb for over six months because of using the stick too soon and putting too much pressure on the newly healed breaks. But after that it was all right, and that was the end of it.

I did feel put upon when I tripped while trying to negotiate the steps into the trailer without sufficient support and gashed and bruised my shin on the sharp metal doorsill. But that was only the beginning. It was soon easy to become convinced that there was someone invisible right behind me for quite a while, trying constantly to upend me.

A broken arm had not kept me from my writing. Fingers in a cast are supposed to be exercised, so I exercised them on the typewriter keys. Although the talkers in my mind had stopped bothering me, because I had kept myself closed to them for so long, I still knew better than to open my mind to Mother to let her reach me that way; but it wouldn't hurt to type with her again, would it? I had been working, ever since arriving in Daytona, on a book about my early life and my first experiences at communication, and it was getting in sufficient shape that it seemed it might be ready for a publisher soon. But help was needed to get Mother's information completed.

Mother turned me over to a new scribe, saying that he had a lot more power than she did to get through to me and also that he knew so much more than she did. He is the one I call James, who eventually revealed himself to me as Dr. William James, the American philosopher and psychologist who died in 1910 and who had been one of the founders of the American Society for Psychical Research. He was a much more forceful communicant than Mother, and he was able to amplify considerably the material she had given me.

James particularly maintained that the large amount of trouble caused by this curious activity of trying to correspond with the spirits of the dead more than made up for the small amount of good that could come from it. If one wanted to attempt communication, he should never do so unless he had sat for a long time in a mediumistic development class, James said; but I was eventually to learn that there are very few of those any more that are dependable.

Such warnings in advance would once have been of great value to me. But it was too late now. I was still under the influence of the fiends, even though I thought that by closing them out of my mind I had rid myself of them. There was a peck of trouble ahead of me yet.

In May, when my broken arm was just about healed, I decided my manuscript was ready to try to find a publisher, and began wondering to whom to send it. Mother wrote on the typewriter that I was going to take it to New York City myself. I had never in my life thought of moving to New York, and certainly now that my money was nearly gone was not the time. She was insistent, however, no matter how much argument she was given. She knew positively that I would be moving there to live very soon, so there was no point in giving her any hassle about it. This was a prediction I was afraid might come true, because New York's size had overpowered me on my only visit there. To think of taking it on alone with no money was appalling.

Of course, I went. It was Junior who proved Mother right. My dear little companion had not been lively for some time and it seemed to me he was showing his age. He was ill, instead. Suddenly his hind legs began to stiffen and he screamed with pain whenever his back was touched; a vet said he had a slipped disc in his spine. This is apparently commonplace in dachshunds, with their low-slung frames. The prognosis was ultimate paralysis, or else an operation that might possibly be successful.

In Alabama, just off the route to New York, was the best veterinary college and hospital in the South, where spinal fusion operations on dachshunds were performed frequently. On hearing about it, I packed the car in a rush and headed for it. Since we were having to go part-way North, might as well go all the way, then; and so my plans included doing exactly what Mother had predicted.

We arrived at the Small Animal Clinic just two days before the head surgeon left for his summer vacation, and Junior underwent a laminectomy the next morning. It was Memorial Day exactly two years from the day Nina had died, and this made it doubly difficult for me as I paced the floor of a motel room. It was the first time in my life that I really prayed to a loving Father God who might have my interest at heart. I'd recently been given so much information about Him by my typewriter communicants that I felt secure in His love and able to ask Him for my pet's life without hesitation.

Junior had a rough time, but he was so sure New York was for him that he pulled through in order not to miss the big adventure with me. It was only two days later that I made a bed in the front seat of the car for the tightly bandaged little fellow and started north. Billie and Bob Feagans, friends of mine from my Oakland days, now lived just outside Lynchburg, Virginia, and we spent ten days with them while Junior recuperated.

When we left their home, a cycle began of non-disastrous accidents that, it soon became obvious, were considerably more than chance. When we drove out of Lynchburg, early one morning, the filling-station operator probably having put extra air in the back tires in order to support our bulging cargo, the heat of the road warmed them and they blew out, one at a time, within two hours. Fortunately, I was able to hang onto the wheel and pull over to the side of the road in each instance. Then a passing Samaritan changed the tire and I went on to the nearest town to buy a new one.

I spent the night with more former Oakland friends, the Joseph Soukups, in Baltimore. The next morning, when I took a shower in their tub I put all my weight on the soap dish to support myself when turning around. It pulled loose from the wall and I crashed to the bottom of the tub. Other than a half-inch cut on my leg and a slightly sore muscle, there was no damage to the body.

The nest day, we bypassed New York City and arrived at the Stamford, Connecticut, home of my friend Jean Fonda, who had once helped me put out my little newspaper in Daytona Beach. After much happy reminiscence about our *Shopping with Susy* days, I retired with Junior to an upstairs bedroom. The dog's bandages had been removed, revealing a bald hide where he had been shaved from his neck to his tail, and a scar that was healing nicely. He was convalescing beautifully, with complete use of his back legs once again and no pain; but I still had to lift him up and down from things and had been warned that he must never again traverse flights of steps.

The next morning, however, he got out of our room ahead of me and started downstairs. Seeing him on the top step, I shrieked for him to stop. This startled him and he lost his balance. As I prayed, "O God, help! Save him, save him!" he fell down the entire flight. But what he did was to slide and skid on the highly waxed stairs and manage to keep upright all the way down. He landed on his feet, and looked up at me from the bottom of the stairs with a rather surprised expression. I know he was thinking, "There must be a better way to do that." Then he stalked into the kitchen and hit Jean for some breakfast.

I found a nice one-room, kitchen, and bath apartment in a big new building in New York City, and after a time with Jean I moved in. The second week there, I fell in the dark, flat on my face through the open bathroom door. And once again, did not hurt myself.

A few days later, I fell off a bus. It was rather unnerving, but nothing was chipped, bruised, or broken.

It was not long afterward that I tripped on the metal strip across the entrance to an old-fashioned elevator in an older building I was visiting and stretched my length on the floor. That time, I hurt a finger slightly.

There obviously was someone protecting me in all these misadventures that did not prove damaging, and I attributed it to my guardian angels. But I also wondered why they could not keep such things from happening to me in the first place. Finally, I sat at my typewriter after giving them a very severe talking to and received the response that they could not protect me in advance unless I co-operated by the proper thinking. It was not easy for them to get new ideas into my head about something I was so closely involved with personally, but eventually I began to receive the concept of wrapping myself mentally in protection, visualizing myself completely covered with the power of my thoughts to defend me. I was later to learn that practically everybody in the psychic field knows of enveloping oneself in "the white Christ light." You mentally enclose yourself in something that acts as a barrier to the intruders. I thought then that it was the power of your belief in its ability to help you that protects you. Now I am more inclined to believe that it is invoking the name of Christ that performs the feat of protection. I have learned that even if you do not believe in the possibility of spirits of the dead intruding themselves upon you, it is wise to hold the certainty always in your mind that as a child of God you are protected from dangers. It doesn't even hurt to say it every time you get into your car for a spin: "I am safe. I am protected by Jesus at all times."

After I was told how to safeguard myself, I spent much of my time visualizing myself wrapped in a protective white light that was all-encompassing and so firm and solid that none of the satanic influences could get inside it and assault me. I maintained that the power of this light was strong enough to protect me, and so it was. All my attacks stopped, and I did not fall any more . . . until I went to Europe and fell off a bus. But that was much later on.

CHAPTER VI

"...Always Learning but Never Able to Reach a Knowledge of the Truth"*

Even though this may not set well with some people, it must be stated that I was prepared for Christianity by my psychical research. I arrived by the back door, so to speak. There was no way my agnostic mind could accept the premises of Christianity until I had convinced myself of the possibility of survival after death. Also, the reality of prophecy, angels, demons, the working of miracles, supernormal healing, and the discerning of spirits had to be proved empirically to my satisfaction before I could accept the resurrected Christ or anything else from Scripture.

Most people become converted or saved and thereby endorse all the premises of Christianity, but there are undoubtedly many others who go about it backward, as I did. My reverse approach was in operation all the time I lived in New York City, as I associated with persons who were also seekers after philosophical and religious answers, and we frequently attended meetings of anything and everything that was going on.

I was determined at first not to take an office job but to make it on my own with my writing. The manuscript I had

* 2 Tim. 3:7 (New American Bible)

brought to New York was not worth publishing, and rejections soon convinced me; so I had to look for work, after all. Fearing the big-city traffic, with its crowded buses and subways, I did not look for a job downtown but inquired instead at Lenox Hill Hospital, which was only two blocks away. I started there in the Admitting Office and later took a secretarial job in the Pathology Laboratory, thus completing a circle that had started while I was convalescing from my hip operation many years before and had learned medical terms and watched surgery in the hospital. After that, I worked as a secretary in the office of four doctors.

It was during this time that I applied to the Parapsychology Foundation for a grant to condense into one volume the huge, two-volume tome *Human Personality and Its Survival of Bodily Death*, by Frederic W. H. Myers. Receiving the sum of two thousand dollars, with two years to accomplish the feat, I worked nights on the condensation and days at the doctors' office. It was finished in time; and then I received another grant, to write a book called *The Mediumship of Mrs. Leonard*. After that appeared, I was on my way as an author and could give up my office job. Believe me, it was a tight financial squeeze for many years; but I was doing what I most wanted to do in all the world, so had no complaints.

During my eight years in New York, I seldom made an effort to communicate with Mother or James. They said the vibrations in the big city were not conducive to that kind of effort. Instead, my spare time was spent investigating every aspect of the psychic and metaphysical that could be found . . . and New York abounds with meetings and churches of all kinds. I joined the Society for Psychical Research (London), the American Society for Psychical Research, the Association for Research and Enlightenment, Spiritual Frontiers Fellowship, and other organizations, and attended development classes with several prominent mediums, the famous Arthur Ford among them.

At that time I started a custom that continued until after I received the Baptism: to have an ESP development class or meditation group meet once a week at my home. Many of such are held without any invocation or prayers; and, always attempting to maintain a parapsychological objectivity, I at first did not encourage praying in my groups. But we found that it was not possible to keep out the negative forces unless we prayed. So we soon came to opening every meeting with the Lord's Prayer. In this way, things stayed under control most of the time.

Even in such orderly groups as ours, however, occasionally there were disruptive forces that came with the guests; and we soon learned to screen applicants for membership carefully. I recall a young man who visited once who was undoubtedly under some kind of demonic influence. He was so atheistic he could not stay in the room when we said the Lord's Prayer, but got up and walked outside instead. Before the evening was over, he went into a trance and was unable to come out of it normally, and it was obvious from the things he said that he was possessed by something of a very evil nature.

Although many groups in the psychic and occult field sit and meditate with few problems of this nature, I mention the possibility because it does often occur. And those who indulge in mind-control courses and Transcendental Meditation should be especially aware of it. For every person who can handle all this wisely, there is probably someone else who will get into trouble because of it. It is true that those who are inclined to be neurotic are particularly attracted to this kind of activity; and who can screen them out before they do harm to themselves and possibly to others?

Most of the precepts of the metaphysical sects I looked into were incompatible with my ideas, and I did not become too deeply involved with them. There is very little of the mystical in my nature, and so Eastern occultism left me cold. Because of my indoctrination, at the Parapsychology Laboratory at Duke, to be objective and critical, I found myself analyzing unfavorably many beliefs and customs that other persons accepted without question, being taken in by the romanticism of them. This is particularly true of reincarnation, which is tremendously popular, but which to me is an appalling concept, destroying all the individuality of the soul or spirit. Some ardent believers have found me a bit difficult because of this.

On the night of September 24, 1976, while writing this book, and a year and a half after I received the Baptism, an experience occurred that brought me an understanding of why I might have been so ready when the time came for my conversion to Christianity. It revealed to me that I had been quite fed up with the field I was in.

When asked to speak on ESP to a singles club in Tucson, I decided to talk instead on the dangers of attempting to communicate with spirits. "Stay away from Ouija boards and automatic writing like the plague," I told the good-sized audience. I related the story of the voices that had spoken in my mind and mentioned the many letters received from persons who had run into similar and even more disastrous problems. During the question-and-answer period afterward, it was revealed that several in the audience had either heard voices in their minds and did not know how to cope with them or knew someone who had. It was a very responsive group.

The first questions asked were from a couple in the front row. The young man stood up and said, "Do you believe in God?"

"Yes," I replied. "Even before I became a Christian, my communicants had told me about a concept of God I could learn to know and love."

The young man then said, "Do you accept Jesus Christ as your Savior?" And I said, "Yes, indeed I do."

Shortly after this, a woman sitting near the rear raised her hand and was acknowledged. "I don't agree with you about using Ouija boards," she said. "I have used mine for years. I know enough to protect myself with the white Christ light and I have had no trouble of any kind."

"I'm glad you've had good results," I replied. "And I know that some others have had similar experiences to yours. But think of all those who don't know enough to protect themselves. They are the ones I particularly wish to warn."

Shortly afterward, a question came up about reincarnation and I stated my position on that, saying that even though most people interested in the occult believe in it, my spirit communicants said it was definitely not so, and I chose to go along with them.

Then the Ouija-board lady jumped up to defend reincarnation. "Don't you know," she said, "that Ruth Montgomery had a book written through her by Arthur Ford just a few weeks after his death? It tells about many famous people and who they are now reincarnated into."

Anyone who knew Arthur Ford was aware that he did not believe in reincarnation. I said that it would be difficult for me to accept the idea that he could, so quickly after his passing, have changed his mind and become interested in where a bunch of famous people had been reborn. I added that it was no use to argue reincarnation, because someday, after we are dead and gone, we will certainly find out the truth about it, and until then the subject no longer interests me.

She insisted, bringing up the many books that have been written in favor of the subject. Even as she continued to talk about it, the Christian woman in the front row began interrupting her. "Listen to Susy," she said. "She's right. It is all dangerous. Listen to her. Listen to her."

I appreciated this confirmation, and since it didn't seem possible to hush the other woman up, I just sat back for a few moments and let them both talk simultaneously, the one in back to those near her who would listen; the one in front to the rest of the audience.

But, on the way home, talking about the incident to the nice young woman who was transporting me, I began to realize that it was the predominance of people like my Ouija-board friend who had turned me off so completely from my former interests. Too many newcomers—and old-timers too, for that matter— have found a metaphysical or Eastern religious concept that intrigued them and decided once and for all that they had the *only* answer. From then on, there was little new they had learned, being so engrossed in their own opinions that they

could accept nothing else. This is a natural human charac-
teristic, and perhaps if I had agreed in principle with these people they would not have irritated me as they did. The problem
was that *everybody* wanted to argue reincarnation with me the
minute they learned that I did not believe in it. I used to argue
right back, but now the subject has, quite frankly, become bor-
ing to me. I realize that it could have been, in large part, the
continued insistence of well-meaning persons like the Ouija
lady that had helped me to be ready to accept Christianity
when my exposure at the charismatic retreat occurred.

I enjoyed living in New York, going to the theater and con-
certs as well as many lectures and meetings. Junior loved it also.
He found so much interesting news in a block's walk that he
looked forward to his daily exercise. But he was getting on toward twelve years old and rather settled in his ways, quite content to stay indoors the rest of the time. For his last year or so,
he had difficulty eating what he liked because of a colitis condition, and finally, in March 1963, I lost my little partner. It
broke my heart.

I needed something to take my mind off my lonesomeness,
so I went to Europe that summer. Someone had told me the
Continent could be done on five dollars a day, but he was
misinformed. Anyway, I broke my foot falling off a bus in Italy
—they have little, three-cornered steps that are just murder—
and so spent most of my time abroad in hospitals. As it had
been about six years since my invasion by tripping and pushing
spooks, I did not blame this on them.

In London, on my way home, I had my most realistic psychic experience: you might say an attack of mediumship hit me
overnight, but it lasted for only one occasion. The ability must
have rubbed off on me from Gladys Osborne Leonard, one of
the two or three greatest mediums in history, about whom I
had written a book. Mrs. Leonard had been studied for over
fifty years by scientific investigators, and every word that had
come through her when she was in trance had been recorded
and analyzed for the survival evidence it provided. She was
never once found to have done anything that in any way in-

dicated fraud or connivance of any kind. In her late seventies at the time she invited me to visit her at her home in Kent, this great Christian lady looked and acted as if she were in her fifties, and she was the most serene person one could meet. I was hoping that some of her tranquillity and composure might be contagious but did not suspect that her mediumship might be.

Back in London the next day, I remembered a chore a New York acquaintance had asked me to do for her. She had given me the name and address of a British woman, whom I'll call Elsie, requesting that I telephone her and inquire why she did not write. She had told me nothing about Elsie, and I had been in England for some days and had not bothered to call her. Now an immediate urge possessed me to phone her. Elsie said she would love to meet me but that her house was in a state of disarray because she was packing to leave the next day for Italy. I truly cared nothing about seeing her but now found myself insisting, "Oh, I won't take but a few minutes of your time." So she said to come on over.

When I walked out of the telephone booth in the lobby of the small hotel in which I was staying, the manager was standing nearby. When asked how to get to Elsie's address, some distance across London, he said, "I'm leaving now in my car and driving right by the house. I'll be glad to give you a lift."

Almost as soon as Elsie greeted me, she began pouring forth her woes to me, and she had many to relate. She'd lost her husband to another woman and, as was legal in England, he had taken all her furniture and valuable family possessions when the divorce was granted. Then her sister had died of cancer. Shortly afterward, one of her beloved twin Siamese cats had fallen from a window and been killed and the other had died of grief.

I felt terribly sorry for Elsie but could hardly listen for the lightheadedness that was overcoming me. I had to lay my head against the back of the couch and soon was in what obviously was a light trance. My mind was conscious, but the rest of me was not functioning. Then a strong impression came that her sister insisted on talking to her.

It was embarrassing to have to ask a strange woman if she wanted her dead sister to speak to her through me. Fortunately, she was receptive. So words began to tumble from my mouth that were in no way instigated by me. As my tongue spoke, my mind listened and was horrified, because there was no way of knowing whether or not what was being said was true. I might be making a monstrous fool of myself.

Through me, Elsie was told to stop grieving so much and talking so much about her difficult experiences.

"When you are in Italy, try not to tell anyone about your problems. Be sure to take your oil paints and spend as much time as possible painting. That will be wonderful therapy for you," I said, having no possible idea whether or not the woman was an artist but realizing that the rest of the advice was sound, even if it might be coming only from my own subsconscious mind.

More went on, which I do not now recall, then my voice said, "Mother and I are with you all the time and love you very much and do all we can to help you. Trust us and make yourself receptive to us."

Cringing, I came out of the trance prepared to slip away unobtrusively if my hostess showed anger or discomfort, but instead she was exultant. "You don't know what you've done for me," she cried. "This is the nicest thing that ever happened to me."

"Was the information correct?" I asked. "Are you an artist? Is your mother dead?"

"Everything you said was true, and the advice was so wise that I promise to follow it," she declared. As she showed me out the door, she was as happy as she had been miserable when she asked me to enter, so it was obvious that what had happened had been a good thing.

It is odd and perhaps rewarding that nothing of this type ever occurred to me again. During all my psychical-research period, I seemed destined to have one of each kind of experience

and no more. It was as if I were supposed to understand it all
from personal experience so that I could become convinced of
the reality of life after death but not get too involved with any
of it.

In the fall of 1965, I signed a contract with World Publishing Company for *Prominent American Ghosts,* for which a
tour of the country was in order. I stored my furniture and
moved from New York City permanently when I left on a Ca-
nadian airplane for Calgary, visited Banff and Lake Louise, and
then took the train on to Seattle, where there was a haunted
school for my book. There was also a medium to investigate,
who was intriguing at first but eventually disappointing. I am
now convinced that he was almost invariably fraudulent. I enjoyed learning to know the beautiful city of Seattle but after
three months left it, with enthusiastic anticipation for Hawaii,
on the next leg of my journey. It had always been a dream of
mine to go there.

After some lectures and several beautiful weeks sight-seeing
throughout the islands, I returned to the mainland, to Los Angeles, to spend the winter. In the spring, I flew to New Orleans,
still on my haunt hunt, and there were several delightful old
houses in the Vieux Carré with wrought-iron decorated bal-
conies and enough ghosts for any taste. Then I went to Gulf-
port, where the house of a prominent doctor had been haunted
for some time. I bought a second-hand Corvair in Mississippi
and drove up the East Coast, ultimately as far as Maine.

I adored Maine, being particularly charmed by the seacoast
towns with their tall elm trees and huge white sea captains'
mansions. And it was there I sent out a couple of prayers that
were so miraculously answered, bringing such quick and specific
results, that they really should be reported here. I was finally
learning how to do it, it seems.

In Saco there was such a deep, penetrating fog that all traffic
had been halted. There was nowhere left in town to spend the
night but one last, lonely, falling-apart tourist camp, depressing
in its gloom. I prayed hard for guidance that night, because I

was at a crossroad, frightened by some of the ghostly situations recently run into, and very blue.

Where to write my book was my main problem. I really wanted to return to California, but my car was not up to such a long drive, and my furniture was stored in New York. It is hard for a person not to have one stationary place to call home, and family to go to in times of need. I had many friends who would put me up, but few of them had room for me for any kind of a long stretch, especially because when I write a book there are mounds of papers strewn all around me for months at a time. Obviously my own thoughts about this were not getting me anywhere, so I put my conflict in God's hands with one of the most sincere, ardent prayers of my life. It was so successful that it gave me a feeling of confidence I'd never had before about His immediate response to needs.

The next morning, I phoned psychic Shirley Harrison, a Saco resident whom I had met in New York. She invited me to her home for lunch, and there I met astrologer and yoga teacher Marcia Moore, who gave me a warm welcome because she was familiar with my work. Then, during our conversation, I mentioned my impasse.

"I've just been on a tour of the country doing research for a book," I said. "But now that I have all the material and am ready to write it, I don't know where to go."

"Come home with me," Marcia said. "I live with my husband, Mark Douglas, in a big house on the coast near York Beach. We could let you have a room and private bath for the rest of the summer."

So I did just that, rooming and boarding there for nearly three months and completing the book during that time. The house was one of those huge, twenty-room "summer cottages" so often built in the early part of the century along the New England seashore. Marcia and Mark and I rattled around in the big place like seeds in a maraca until her children came home for a vacation.

Frankly, I found the house spooky, because I was writing about ghosts and it was so big and so empty and so hauntable.

There were never any ghostly occurrences there, and as I sat at my typewriter looking out at the ocean during the daytime, I was very happy. When the tides went out at dusk, my back (which was exposed to the large bedroom and the larger hallway beyond my open door and the still more immense stairwell on beyond, that reached clear to the yawning attic) began to chill. I closed my door, turned on the lights, worked hard to control my mind, and still felt creepy.

"What a dumb profession I'm in," I moaned. "Why do publishers always insist that I write about ghosts and such?"

When September came, the book was finished and off to the publisher. Mark and Marcia were soon going to close the house for the winter. And where was Susy to move from Maine? There was really no desire to go back to New York, get my furniture out of storage, and start out in the rat race once again. It seemed as if I were always having to ask, "Where do I go now?" And it was obvious that I had to have special help about it. Even though I was now trying to live my life as if God were a part of it, sometimes when big decisions must be made, even more prayerful effort had to be expended in order to get specific results.

So I expended mightily for several days. The response came so promptly as to be miraculous: a letter from Margaret Sanders Adams, who was planning a trip around the world for about six months and wondered if I might like to live in her Miami penthouse apartment while she was away. Naturally, my acceptance was immediate. So Margaret and I met in New York to attend a meeting of the Parapsychological Association; then we went to Maine to sell my car and get my things. Two days later, we were on the way to Miami in Margaret's Mercedes-Benz, which was then at my disposal until her return from her world tour.

Miami was nice, and so, after Margaret came back, I took an apartment of my own and remained there. Fortunately, an established writer can let his agent cope with the New York problems and is free to live where he wants to. I wrote several books while in Miami, but the most curious one came to me in a highly unusual manner, at a time when I just happened to have nothing particularly pressuring me and life was calmly pleasurable. It had been long since I had made any effort to communicate with Mother or James, but I felt sure they were around, giving me their guardian angelship when necessary.

On Wednesday, February 22, 1967, I had dinner at the home of my friend Anne Fansler, and then we rested quietly and meditated for a while. As we were sitting there, we began to have an unusually elated feeling, as if something exciting were about to happen; then a voice began to speak through my lips, not of my own volition. It apparently was James, for he gave a message of commendation and inspiration and then said that if I would meet him at my typewriter the next morning at nine o'clock, he would begin to write the book he wanted to give me.

Every day for the next week, I sat at my typewriter most of the time, and in that one week the entire book was written through me. Since I take a week or sometimes longer to write one chapter on my own, the speed with which this came convinced me that it was not accomplished in any way by myself alone. The material was rather wordy, as most alleged spirit writing is, for it is apparently difficult for the communicant always to get the right meaning he wants through the typist's mind. So, after that, for years, whenever there was any spare time, I would work with James at the typewriter, editing his material and getting it ready for eventual publication.

The information James gave was an amplification of what had been given originally by Mother and labeled "Mother's Chapter." It told about conditions in life after death, denied the reality of reincarnation, and spoke of the importance of controlling one's thinking and loving one's fellow men. James did not go in for anything mystical or of an oriental flavor, and this sat well with my strictly occidental mind. This book did more than anything else to convince me of the reality of life after death. With it I came to the conclusion that I had it made philosophically and religiously and there was no need to seek further.

After three years in Miami, I lived in Mexico for a while, then returned to New York City, in the spring of 1970, and signed the contract for *Confessions of a Psychic*. I spent the summer in an apartment in Oakland, Maryland, working on that book; but, by fall, I was ready to find a place to live where the climate liked aching bones. So I undertook another trek westward, ending up in San Diego, California.

At Christmas that year, I received a card from Salt Lake City from my old friend Veryl Smith, now Mrs. Karl Romer, saying she and her husband would be touring in their Cortez motor home and would see me sometime in January. Although they specified no date, my ESP was working on January 14, for I looked for them all day. It was not until the next morning that Veryl phoned.

"Where were you yesterday?" I asked her. "I was expecting you then."

"We were here, but it was raining too hard to get out to phone you," she replied.

The Romers stayed a week and listened to me read my finished manuscript. This was a great favor to me, because I always feel the need to read aloud before being sure a book is just as it should be, and I did not know any people in San Diego well enough to ask them to listen.

After the Romers left, I did not hear from them again. In April I had muscle spasms in my back so bad that I rushed for the desert to dry them out of me. Ending up in Tucson, I made a down payment on a large double mobile home, put it in the best court in town, with a swimming pool right across a grassy lawn from me, and realized the place to put down my roots had finally been found. For once this was true. I have lived here and loved it ever since.

The interesting coincidence that made me feel God had a hand in it: when I wrote the Romers in May of my move to Tucson, Veryl answered that they had just returned from there, where they, too, planned to settle down on a lot they had bought, just fourteen miles north of town.

Jean Fonda, now widowed, and her mother have also moved

to Tucson. Many wonderful new friends have come to me here, but it is especially nice to have such good old friends nearby.

So here I was in 1975, quietly existing in my comfortable home in a salubrious climate. I wasn't exactly happy, but I thought that was all there was for me and I was making the best of it, ready to retire in a year, ready to die with few qualms when it became necessary. I was also . . . ready for Jesus. I did not know it; but the Lord did, when He arranged for me to attend that charismatic retreat at Picture Rocks.

CHAPTER VII

"...Speaking in Tongues and Glorifying God"*

But what is this charismatic renewal movement that opened the door to Christianity for me? I was to learn that it is a recent and rapidly growing phenomenon in the church which has become so widespread that its members are now in the hundreds of thousands all over the world, transcending denominational barriers in all nations. As John Sherrill says in *They Speak with Other Tongues*, "The breath of the living God is stirring" today.

Although I was introduced to it through the Catholics, it is becoming just as active among Episcopalians, Methodists, Lutherans, etc. It is already traditional in Pentecostal and Assembly of God churches. Father Richard Schiblin, who led the first retreat I attended, said that there is not much difference between the charismatic movement among Catholics and that among main-line Protestant churches. His center is very ecumenical, he told me, and weekly prayer meetings there are attended by many non-Catholics.

Receiving the Baptism in the Holy Spirit and being born again is the goal of the charismatic, and with it comes a happiness in worship that is seldom found among Christians who have not had that experience. "Religion must fill the heart

* Acts 10:46 (New American Bible)

with life and joy or it is nothing," says Dr. Marcus Bach in *The Inner Ecstasy*. And that is why there is so much appeal to becoming a charismatic.

Another statement about this I appreciate is in *Charismatic Bridges*, by Vinson Synan:

> Probably one of the greatest reasons for the phenomenal growth of the pentecostal and charismatic movements around the world is the joy that is evident in pentecostal worship. People are attracted to life, not to dead forms. Life responds to life. The church must find a way of making emotion in worship respectable again if it is to survive. Shouts of joy and ecstasy are quite respectable at a ball game or a rock concert, but never in church! When did the church lose its pristine joy? At what point did it become indecorous to praise God in his sanctuary? What theologian or ecclesiastical functionary gave ecstasy a bad name? It is high time to restore the joy of the Lord to our liturgies and grant seasons of praise to the millions who are starving to worship the Lord "in Spirit and in truth."

When I first heard the word "charismatic" I immediately thought of John F. Kennedy, because it, in its definition of "charm," had so frequently been applied to him. I was to learn that the term comes from the Greek word "charisma" and basically it means a spiritual gift from God—"a spark of divine energy and inspiration." The simple gifts of faith, hope, and love are the most important, but emphasis is also placed on the more exotic gifts, such as prophecy, healing, and speaking in tongues. More specifically, the charismata are the gifts that descended upon the disciples on the day of Pentecost as described in Acts 2:4 ff (New American Bible). At that time, "All were filled with the Holy Spirit" and began to express themselves in foreign tongues that they did not know and to "make bold proclamations as the Spirit prompted them" and to speak "about the marvels God has accomplished." It was this great ex-

perience that jolted the disciples out of their inertia caused by
Jesus' death and so renewed them that they became highly mo-
tivated and successful missionaries.

Dr. Henry Pitney Van Dusen, former president of New
York's Union Theological Seminary, once wrote in *Life* magazine that the Holy Spirit—so neglected by many traditional
Christians—is "the immediate, potent presence of God both in
each human soul and in the Christian fellowship."

Praying in the Spirit, or praying in tongues, helps you to talk
to God through your spirit instead of your mind. "It'll come up
over your tongue," says Oral Roberts, in *Abundant Life*, "just
like your English language, and God will speak back to your
mind and you'll then have the tongue of understanding. . . .
That's why praying in the Spirit is an important piece of the
whole armor of God."

Technically, the term for praying in tongues is "glossolalia,"
but it seems to be seldom used among those who produce it.
They call it "tongue-speaking" or "prayer language." Those
who have had the Baptism do it often in private and occasionally in church and prayer meetings, but in my experience it
is seldom a wild, "Holy Roller" kind of thing. What I had read
about it and seen of it previous to my personal encounters with
it led me to believe that the people who did it went into some
kind of light trance and were spoken through by spirits; but
this is not so. As Father Dick Schiblin told me, "When I do it,
I'm conscious of what I'm doing. I start it and stop it."

Stories have been told about people, actually possessed by an
evil spirit, who were blaspheming God in some obscure African
dialect when they thought they were praising Him in tongues.
If this does occur, it is probably very infrequent.

Some people do not speak in tongues at all, even though
they have had the Baptism in the Holy Spirit. They are somehow unwilling to let themselves go to that extent. They probably would try to learn to do it if they realized just how fulfilling
it is. Speaking in tongues is actually a way to glorify God without letting your thoughts and words get in the way.

Dr. Van Dusen told John Sherrill it was "a kind of spiritual therapy . . . an emotional release of an ultimately healthy kind. It left people better off: released, relaxed."

And St. Paul said, "He who prays in an unknown tongue edifies himself." (I Corinthians 14:4, King James)

Glossolalia is prayer talk, plain and simple. It sounds definitely like a language, with intonations and emphasis, but in most cases it is merely an accumulation of nonsense syllables. John Dart and Russell Chandler, in "Speaking in tongues: Is it all religious?" in the Los Angeles *Times*, say that William Samarin, a linguist of the University of Toronto, made an extensive study of tongue-speaking on several continents over a five-year period. He concluded that the recorded segments he had on file were "always strings of syllables made up of sounds taken from among all those that the speaker knows, put together more or less haphazardly but which nevertheless emerge as word-like and sentence-like units because of realistic language-like rhythm and melody." He saw it as a valid and authentic religious experience.

Rev. Morton Kelsey, an Episcopal charismatic, has called it "a breakthrough into the consciousness from the objective psyche, or the deep collective level of the unconscious."

There are those who maintain instead that it is completely and entirely the Holy Spirit speaking through you and that there is no other explanation. This would undoubtedly seem to be true on certain occasions at least, especially when there is specific prophecy. Frequently in church services of the Pentecostal type or in prayer meetings, an individual stands up and gives a message in tongues. This is often quite disconcerting to the novice who observes it, because the speaker may sound overly dramatic and pretentious. Then someone else gives an interpretation in English. But when the prophecy is accurate and the event comes to pass, it is hard not to be convinced that something supernormal is involved.

St. Paul said, "For he that speaketh in an unknown tongue speaketh not unto men, but unto God: for no man understandeth him. . . ." (I Corinthians 14:2, King James)

And yet there are occasions, as at the first Pentecost, when the tongues can be understood by others: "Staying in Jerusalem at the time were devout Jews of every nation under heaven. . . . The whole occurrence astonished them. They asked in utter amazement, 'Are not all of these men who are speaking Galileans? How is it that each of us hears them in his native tongue?'" (Acts 2:5 ff, New American Bible)

During altar calls, when people may be lined up awaiting healing or Baptism in the Holy Spirit, there are numerous accounts of foreign languages having been spoken that were recognized by someone present as bringing him a specific message. The Reverend Dennis Bennett, an Episcopal charismatic leader who has been in the movement since 1960, and his wife, Rita, give a good instance in *The Holy Spirit and You:*

They tell of a young Christian who had married a Japanese girl while stationed in Japan with the armed forces. Having returned to the United States with his bride, he took her to a Full Gospel church in Oregon, but she prayed her Buddhist prayers even while he was praying to God through Jesus Christ. "Next to them was kneeling a middle-aged woman, a housewife from the community," the Bennetts say. This woman began to pray aloud in tongues, and the Japanese bride suddenly seized her husband's arm:

"'Listen!' she whispered in excitement. 'This woman speak to me in Japanese! She say to me: "You have tried Buddha, and he does you no good; why don't you try Jesus Christ?" She does not speak to me in ordinary Japanese language, she speak temple Japanese, and use my whole Japanese name, which no one in this country knows!' It is not surprising that the young lady became a Christian!"

Another illustration of tongue-speaking that brings a message to someone who is least expecting it is related by Harold Hill in *How to Live Like a King's Kid.* He writes:

> When another man came and sat in the prayer chair, I laid hands on him and prayed for him in the Spirit, praying in tongues. When the prayer was over,

the scoffer was blubbering like a baby, crying up a storm, slobbering all over his expensive blue serge suit.

"What ails you?" I asked.

"Well," he said, "I don't know if the man in the chair got anything, but God spoke to me when you prayed for him, because you were praying in High German. I'm a student of High German, and I doubt if even you know it, because it's a rare language."

I said, "I don't know any German, high, low or medium."

"Well," he said, "God spoke to me in perfect High German and said, *Who are you to scoff at any of My gifts?*" And that big blubbering man got saved, and the next day, I heard him praying for someone in a new language. He was really turned on.

The Spirit will always witness to Jesus.

Don Basham tells, in A *Handbook on Tongues, Interpretation and Prophecy*, of a man he knew who was the speaker at a Christian meeting. "At one point he stopped his message and began speaking in tongues. This was immediately followed by an interpretation of the tongue by someone in the audience. Then the man resumed his message. After the service, a Frenchman came up to the speaker and told him that the message in tongues was in the French language and that the interpretation that followed had been a perfect translation in English of what had been spoken in French. But neither the speaker nor the interpreter knew any French."

Whatever speaking in tongues is, or whatever its source, everyone who has tried it agrees that your life tends to take a whole new turn when you begin to experience it. I was to discover that this is true, and that it is a joyous pouring forth of praise from my inner being. I might liken it to the way the trills and chirps and rolls of melody pour forth from the mouth of a mockingbird. It is prayer, beyond doubt, but a glorifying of God without words getting in the way.

When you are praying, you can say, "Praise God" or "Praise

the Lord" or "Praise You, Jesus," just so many times; then you realize that words are inadequate for the love and joy you feel. And sometimes you want to pray and yet you don't know exactly what to pray about. If you start petitioning, you can repeat your own needs just so often and then you begin to feel as if you are begging. You can thank God just so many times for your blessings, and even for your misfortunes, from which you can grow and learn, but then you begin to be embarrassed. In other words, praying in your own language is a conscious process in which you really would rather your consciousness were not so involved, because sooner or later you become self-conscious. As Oral Roberts says, "Most people pray with their minds. They try to think up the words and don't always think up the words they like."

But when you pray in tongues, you just let your soul hang loose along with your tongue, and the sounds come spouting forth from your mouth in a heavenly language. At the same time, you hold up your hands in supplication, and they seem to act as an antenna or a funnel to channel God's love into your heart and yours to Him.

CHAPTER VIII

"The Time Has Come
for You to Wake..."*

When I attended the retreat at Picture Rocks, I knew nothing about the charismatic movement or the Baptism in the Holy Spirit; and what I thought I knew about speaking in tongues was all wrong. So I just played the whole thing by ear and observed what was going on with mixed emotions and many arguments in my mind. But, as I said in the first chapter, I soon realized that here was what had been missing in all my long lifetime of seeking. And I yearned for more of it.

Many at the retreat had already had the Baptism and were just coming for a renewal among congenial people. Others were interested in trying to receive the Baptism. And still others, like Fay Peters and me, had just come to observe, having been told it would be an interesting and enlightening experience. I particularly appreciated the fact that all of us were treated the same, with nothing pushed at us—no theology and no dogmatic statements. We were allowed to participate as much or as little as we wished, without being pressured in any way.

We tried to learn what we could from everyone we talked to. Before the session was over, I interviewed Father Dick as well. He started telling me of his own charismatic conversion by saying that it began as the result of a "downer." Not being quite

* Rom. 13:11 (Good News for Modern Man)

as up on current terminology as I thought, I said with a start, "You took drugs?" But he had meant, instead, that he was depressed.

"I was in the priesthood but was beginning to get very disillusioned," he said. "Many Christians have been searching for a deeper faith, something they knew should be there, and I was one of them." He attended a private retreat in an old mission in California, and, he said, "The first day of this retreat, it seemed abundantly clear to me that the Lord wanted me to stay where I was as a priest. So I spent the next three or four days at the retreat simply saying a very simple prayer: 'I can't do it. I'm worn out. I can't do it. You've got to do it for me.'"

It was about three days later that a religious sister invited him to a conference on charismatic renewal for the clergy. "I'd heard about speaking in tongues before, but I didn't like it," he said. "I didn't understand it. But I went and was really deeply moved by the whole thing. Then I started attending a charismatic prayer meeting, and one of the first things this group did was ask me to go on a retreat with them—a weekend down in the Santa Cruz Mountains. I went."

Father Dick was at that time writing his sermons out in full in advance, and he went with the understanding that he would have to leave in time to prepare his sermon for Sunday morning. Then he began to realize that on his return home there would be so little time to write it that he asked the group on the retreat to pray over his sermon for him. They did. But even though he left relatively early, he arrived home too late to write his sermon that night. He decided to get up the next morning and do it before the service. "But I overslept," he said, "and just barely got to the church before the service began. Just before it came time to preach, I bowed over to say a prayer and said to the Holy Spirit, 'You've really got to help me this morning.' Just then, the choir started singing the very same hallelujahs the charismatic group had sung when they were praying over me the night before. This really got my attention, because I had never heard them before in a Catholic church. In that moment, a voice that was so clear—and it still is so clear and real to me—said very simply, 'Can you doubt that I am with you?'

"And I knew it was the Lord. He was with me, and it was exactly the word that I needed—that He was with me—and I preached on that. I don't remember what I said, but many people remarked about how beautiful it was. And since then, I've been involved in the charismatic movement."

Priests are usually assigned to a parish. In the fall of 1974, just shortly before the retreat where we met, Father Schiblin asked to be released for full-time charismatic work.

He and I discussed questions I had about various aspects of the movement, as I had observed it there. Then I said, "I don't know about the speaking in tongues or the other specific areas, but I do know that the love and the warmth and the sense of renewal one gets here is going to change the world if it takes over."

Father Dick said, "The Lord said, 'By this shall they know that you are my disciples, that you love one another,' and to me that's always been the most striking thing about the renewal. Just that, not the tongues. To someone who first comes, they may seem very funny, but the thing that really strikes them is the love."

He was very, very right.

A friend, Georgeanna Grusing, of Burlington, Colorado, wrote in her Christmas 1976 newsletter of her similar reaction to a Methodist Holy Spirit conference she attended in Dallas. There, she says, "They had a good hand-clapping, knee-slapping, toe-tapping music that makes me feel ten feet tall, like I could tackle the whole world. But the Spirit went much deeper than the music—power, faith, love, inspiration, healings, peace."

Needless to say, both Fay and I left the retreat with many new ideas and many questions. Being constituted the way I am, I immediately set out to try to find the answers. My first step was to contact the Harrisons, a couple previously met at Spiritual Frontiers Fellowship meetings. They had been pointed out to me as somewhat "far out" because they attended Pentecostal churches, and I had smiled superiorly on hearing it. Now I wanted to see what could be learned from Pentecostal churches, because they are one denomination where, traditionally, there have been speaking in tongues and the Baptism in the Holy Spirit, which, I had begun to realize, are the whole secret to the renewal I sought.

Captain William J. Harrison, D.D.S., U. S. Navy (retired), and his wife, Mary, R.N., had been seeking just as I had for many years. Their research in most cases had been much more in depth than mine. I would look at an organization, a metaphysical group, or a doctrine, read a few of its precepts, and decide it was not for me. They would join up with it and spend maybe a year studying it before going on to something possibly more advanced. Thus their personal knowledge of the whole occult scene was as broad as my knowledge of the psychic field. And yet it was only when they had the Baptism in the Holy Spirit that they really found the answers that satisfied them.

Mary told me about their seeking: "In each metaphysical research it would be as if we finally came to a closed door and it could take us no farther. We found that Jesus was the only one who could."

The Harrisons were visiting various churches and prayer meetings, and I started going with them. I had not known of the many books that have been written about born-again experiences, but the Harrisons introduced me to them, lending me stacks which kept my evenings busy as I read intently, hoping to find explanations that would satisfy me.

And every night, I argued with God in my prayers, telling Him what I could and could not accept. It was the idea of Jesus as *the* Son of God that particularly bothered me. I was having difficulty thinking of Him as anything more than a Big Brother and the greatest Man Who ever lived. I believed, and still do believe, that all men are sons of God, and I could not then make any further distinction in favor of Jesus.

And so I read and argued and wondered and yearned during a period of two months. I also suffered.

Someone has said that the Lord gives us a taste of Hell in our lives so that we can be sure we don't want to go there. Perhaps that is the answer to why things began to pile up on me so hard during this time; but I made up my mind about not going to Hell a long time ago, so it is not easy to be sure just what began happening to me. Anyway, several extremely difficult situations arose in my life during the spring of 1975, when I was contemplating trying to become a spirit-filled Christian. It finally became of concern to me that while I was allowing myself to reach out to new ideas and new religious concepts, my receptivity was opening me up to dangers as well. Even though I do not believe in *the* Devil as a specific individual with powers akin to God, I do know of the influence of devilish spirits, and when I was most vulnerable—when my guard was down, so to speak—perhaps they were ganging up on me.

Then again, maybe the Lord was trying to show me that I couldn't be successful alone—that I needed Him. Perhaps my ego had to be gotten out of the way completely. I had to be practically whipped right down to the ground in order to make me understand that doing it my way was not the answer. Whatever the cause, I learned several very good lessons that spring.

Among such things as an extremely bad financial situation for a while, there were two incidents that particularly bothered me. I was asked to appear on a local television talk show with two other members of the Society of Southwestern Authors. Now, I have been on nationwide TV enough to feel myself at least a semipro at this, and I certainly know better than to act like a prima donna. But, that day, I pestered the technicians about camera angles—something I never do. And what I said while on the air sounded as if I were bragging about myself and my books. On the way home, thinking over the past half hour and realizing what an ass I'd made of myself, I went into a "downer" of my own. I had not had myself under complete control during that broadcast, and it was humiliating to realize it. I was in a deep depression over it for at least a week.

About this time, a man I had met several times (we'll call him Larry) began to phone me for dates. (Yes, older people have romances. We're just as young as anybody in our minds and hearts.) He was a most attractive person, loaded with personality, and most companionable; but, too quickly, I began to think romantically about him in response to his ardor. I knew nothing should come of this, especially since the more he came around, the more it seemed evident that he was considerably younger than I. It also became obvious that he had many irresponsible ways, and he even lied to me on occasion. Nonetheless, I went to Mother with my problems, as in the days of yore. I had seldom made any effort to talk with my spirit friends since James's book was completed, but I cleared my channels of communication as in the past and felt confident that Mother was on the "line" before beginning to query her about Larry. In response, the voice speaking in my mind and claiming to be Mother went into ecstasies!

"This is the man you have always waited for," she said. "He has a great deal of character and you will discover that he is wise and strong. He will not let your physical handicaps stand in his way, and will give you the strength and dependability you have been seeking in a man."

My own instincts told me this was untrue, and the more I saw of Larry the more sure I was of it. But imagine my inner conflict when Mother had given him such a build-up! So I checked with James. Now, in the past, glimpses of the truth were received from James. The high caliber of the material he had sent through me was proof of that. The experience I now had with him, and also with Mother, does not disturb my faith in the veracity of my past communications with them. But, obviously, at the time of this appeal to them my channels were completely blocked. It could very well be that demons or evil spirits were talking to me in their guise even though I had thought the way cleared for safe communication. For James told me exactly the same thing: how right Larry was for me.

Even with this testimony in his favor, which so conflicted with the testimony of my own observations, I decided to be sensible and call the whole thing off before it got out of hand. This I did, and was immediately relieved of all my mental agitation, which need not have occurred had I not attempted once again to contact the spirits. It proved to me that even the most genuine-seeming efforts at communication may be dangerous— to one's morale if nothing else. I have never tried to reach either Mother or James since then and do not intend to do so in the future. I know they understand my reasons. I have also broken up and thrown into the trash the Ouija board and the tin trumpet I still owned but had seldom used in recent years.

During all this time, I was having paroxysms of pain in my right upper arm in the spot where the streptococcal blood poisoning had first struck many long years ago. It had not hurt for ages, but, now that I was on crutches again for my arthritic knees, that muscle was somehow being overworked, causing it to go into spasm. One Friday near the end of April, it had felt as if a sharp knife were sticking into my arm all evening. Much ordinary Tylenol had not relieved it, and I was trying to resist taking Tylenol 4, which has codeine in it. So I was lying in bed reading a book about Jesus and the Baptism in the Holy Spirit and trying to "psych" myself out of the pain. I talked to it and told it to go away, insisting that every cell in my arm and body was filled with God's light and love. I told myself pain was not necessary to get attention—that was available in ample measure. I said Mommy loved me just as much whether or not my arm was hurting. All to no avail.

Finally I laid down the book and said, "Well, all right then, *Jesus*, will you please stop this pain?" It stopped instantly! And it has never come back!

Needless to say, after that dramatic experience I was ready! I realized that Jesus was the magic my life needs. I wanted Him to be my Savior and accepted Him wholeheartedly. All my intellectualizations of religion had never achieved anything like what the spirit-filled people had, and so I decided to stop my arguing and just accept, realizing finally that one must go as a little child, as the Bible says. I didn't want an intellectual religion, to be analyzed and dissected. I wanted an emotional religion, to enjoy.

Catherine Marshall is quoted in *They Speak with Other*

Tongues as saying that you can't approach Christianity through your mind. "It's one of the peculiarities of Christianity that you cannot come to it through intellect," she said. "You have to be willing to experience it first, to do something you don't understand—and then, oddly enough, understanding often follows."

That is the way it finally was with me. I told the Harrisons I was ready, and at the Glad Tidings Assembly of God Church, on the last Sunday in April, I responded to the altar call and received the Baptism in the Holy Spirit. It is true that many people have tried for years without success to get the Baptism. Perhaps it was because I was in such a completely receptive mood that it came to me on my first try. During the time that the minister was holding my hands and praying over me in tongues, I blacked out for an instant. This was the moment when I let myself go completely and accepted the knowledge of my oneness with God, with Jesus, and with the Holy Spirit. I spoke in tongues briefly and very hesitatingly, then began to cry and to quiver inwardly as well as outwardly. Even after returning to my seat, I shook for about half an hour and was in a state of complete exhilaration for hours afterward.

How can I explain the feeling that has remained with me ever since? I had accepted intellectually for some years my oneness with God but, when meditating on that idea, had never had more than a pleasant feeling of what I thought was His inward presence. Now, all the time, I have a glow of happiness that can be switched into high gear by prayer, by reaching up my arms and saying, "Praise You, Lord" or "Bless You, Jesus" or "Praise You, Holy Spirit" or, most especially, by speaking in tongues in the privacy of my bedroom.

I do not expect tongue-speaking to happen to anyone else the way it happened to me, for it seems to vary with each individual. I am not holding myself up as an example. When I went through the Baptism, a few unknown syllables came to my tongue, but I was too embarrassed to let them really sound forth in public. For several nights thereafter, I prayed with happy expectations of a new language streaming from my lips, but nothing came. I complained of this to Mary Harrison, and she said that sometimes one had to sort of "prime the pump" to get it started. I tried this a few times, feeling very foolish even though I was alone, verbalizing a number of odds and ends of sounds. Finally, all of a sudden, the flow started, and then what came was *not* of my own volition; and if what was said was words, it was not any words that I knew or, to my knowledge, had ever heard spoken. Although my pillow talk with God sounds like real conversation, I have never identified it as any language known to me, and I have what might be called a nodding acquaintance with German, Spanish, Italian, Latin, and English.

But, having talked in trance, in near trance, in semitrance, and in other mind-altered situations, I know that it is not some spirit using me as a channel. It seems instead more a matter of my subconscious mind being involved. Perhaps it is sometimes the Holy Spirit speaking through me. As will be seen in a subsequent chapter, I was to become certain that He spoke to me in tongues on at least one occasion and possibly more.

I am not yet clear about many aspects of my religion and still have numerous questions. But I am learning day by day, and it is all beautiful and joyful. To have had the Baptism and to be able to accept the Holy Spirit flowing into me has been the greatest experience of my life. I know now for sure that I am God's property and that He loves me. As St. Paul says (Ephesians 1:13, Good News), ". . . and God put his stamp of ownership on you by giving you the Holy Spirit He had promised."

CHAPTER IX

"It Is Not Good... to Be Alone"*

The knowledge that one belongs to God could make all the difference between feeling alone and feeling a part of the whole, wonderful world. Taking the Jesus route gives you the awareness of His constant companionship, because you are always plugged in to external and eternal forces. If I may be really slangy about it—that's where the action is.

It seems that my main theme throughout my existence has been a loneliness that was never really overcome until Jesus came into my life. If my story were of one who had her conversion from major sin or depravity, this might be a more exciting book. But offhand I would guess that there are more lonely people than sinners to whom I can relate. To them can be said that when Jesus came into my heart and I recognized His place in my daily experience, He moved into my home with me and has given me the fellowship I have always been seeking. Even as I write this, I find it difficult to believe—it's as if something magical has occurred in my life.

Friends have occasionally said that the reason I have never found a man to suit me is that my standards are too high. And it is true that after my first bad experience no man would satisfy me as a permanent partner who did not have intelligence and a great sense of the joy of life. Listen, if even yet the Lord

* Gen. 2:18 (New American Bible)

wants to send me such a companion in the flesh, I'll not complain; but until then my religion is giving me the consolation, the comfort, that makes living alone a pleasure instead of a chore. Even if I only say, "Praise You, Lord" in appreciation of some beautiful music I am hearing on the radio or "Thank You, Jesus" when I get an unexpected royalty check in the mail, I am aware of His presence constantly.

One of the features of a charismatic retreat, at least as it is run by the priests of the Oakland Holy Redeemer Center, is what is called "healing of memories," in which one searches his soul for bad experiences in the past that he needs to recall and replace with thoughts of love and forgiveness, to himself and others. I had done this for myself on several occasions some years before. One night when I was living in New York City and was feeling especially blue, I was wondering why I had always had to be alone for every major event in my life—travels, operations—all the times when most people have companionship.

I was dallying briefly with the idea of reincarnation at that time. I began to wonder if in a past life I had been so popular that now my isolation was in retaliation. Or had a past life been so malicious that now I must suffer for it? I found myself rejecting these ideas and deciding to try to psychoanalyze myself, turning inward, if possible, to events in this life. Perhaps something could be dug up that might be responsible. So in my thoughts I went back, back, back through various lonely or traumatic episodes, clear to my earliest childhood. I came at last to a previously unremembered time when I was only two years old, while Mother had typhoid fever and Daddy moved next door with me to a big old boardinghouse. I could plainly see myself sitting halfway up on a wide staircase which was completely dark. There was no light either in the hall above or below, and I had apparently chosen this as a spot to hide with my unhappiness. In my baby mind I was thinking what a bad girl I must be for my mother to have sent me away from her. I didn't know what I had done that was so naughty, but it must have been something terrible. As I cried out my anguish there on that dark staircase, I also cried as an adult remembering and realized that this rejected baby had set an unconscious mood of loneliness that had never really left me.

Also, my childhood experience of being abandoned, crying on a street corner, when Mother was taken in an ambulance to that same hospital where Daddy was already a patient certainly left its mark on me. I wouldn't be surprised if my many illnesses and hospitalizations throughout my life might not have stemmed from that period of unconscious acceptance of a hospital as a goal to achieve in order to get away from my loneliness and be with my parents. My late friend Bill Hanemann said, "Susy goes to the hospital like anyone else goes to the A & P." And, of course, he was right. I do.

Reminiscence about several of the most unutterably lonely moments of my life brings back episodes that are not pleasing to recount. But it seems to me that the important fact must be brought out that if I had known Jesus, they never would have occurred.

Bill Hanemann had been chief among the fun folk involved with me in putting out my little *Shopping with Susy* tabloid newspaper in Daytona Beach, in the early fifties. He contributed a column of wit and humor, just because he delighted in writing amusing things and seeing them published. He was a former Hollywood writer who had produced the script for Fred Astaire's *Flying Down to Rio*, among other successful movies. In Daytona he and his wife ran a restaurant that advertised with us, and he dropped by almost daily to cause a bit of commotion.

Jean Fonda and Pat Eells, who are still very dear to me, helped me produce the paper in my home, which was more like a clubhouse than an office. Bill referred to it as a salon of distinction because of the many diverting people who congregated there. But if there were any single men in Daytona Beach during the time I was there, they stayed hidden from me. And no matter what good company married men are when they drop in to chat with a bunch of girls putting out a newspaper, the proper ones always go home to their wives, come eventide. So holi-

days were often a menace. I can recall a few of the most miserable moments of my life occurring then just because of being so
completely alone.

One Christmas Eve, I made calls on several people early in
the evening. I found myself with Jean's family at just about
the time they were starting to open their gifts and have their
little private celebration, so of course I did not stay. But I
couldn't bring myself to go home and be alone all the rest of
the evening. So I went to a cocktail lounge . . . where I felt
completely out of place on Christmas Eve. As I sat there trying
to make casual conversation with the bartender, I realized that
not one of the men lined up along the bar was having a word
to say. As I looked down the row of morose faces, I said to myself, "Poor people, nowhere to go on Christmas Eve but a
bar." Suffering for all those others as well as for myself, I found
that tears were flowing into my vodka and tonic, or scotch and
soda . . . or whatever. Nobody even noticed, for each person
there was completely immersed in his own gloom. As I paid my
check and walked out, wishing everyone a "Merry Christmas,"
I was still sobbing bitterly, and I went home and cried myself
to sleep.

A girl friend and her mother had invited me for Christmas
dinner, so the next day was pleasant. *They* had been to a can-
dle-lighting service at their church the night before; but such a
thing had never even occurred to me.

In Maryland, before I went to work for the Oakland newspaper, I had always been trying to get away from Mother's
apron strings. She was the nicest person imaginable, but also
the most dictatorial. Much as she loved me, she had never realized I was grown and continually tried to run my life for me,
especially when she saw what a mess I made of it on my own.

So I contacted the Maryland Vocational Rehabilitation Service for a job, and they were able to get me what seemed to be
an excellent one in Baltimore. I was to be the secretary to the
director of nursing at the Union Memorial Hospital. Even
though my shorthand was not great, my knowledge of medical
terms and hospital routine was enough to qualify me. But it

turned out that the reason someone from out of town was hired for that position was that no one else would remain there because of the arrogance of the head nurse, for whom I worked.

My job was to get the special-duty nurses on and off each day's cases. I made a point to memorize their names the first time I met them, and they were intrigued by this. So they started chatting with me as they came in for work; occasionally we ate together in the hospital cafeteria, and some of them invited me to their homes. Since I was alone in a city where I knew no one, this was most gratefully received. But, several months later, all the nurses froze up on me and would have nothing to do with me. What had I done to offend them? I wondered, melancholy at this unkind treatment. I eventually learned that the head nurse had decided they were becoming too friendly with me and had issued an ultimatum that no nurse was to fraternize with the "hired help"—namely me. She observed the caste system so thoroughly that she believed nurses talked only to doctors and doctors talked only to God.

During the time that I was ostracized without knowing why, an experience occurred that I later learned was amusing. It did not seem so at the time. The Vocational Rehabilitation Service, realizing that I needed help to adjust to my job situation, sent me to a psychiatrist. And he wore a hearing aid! It is not easy to bring yourself to reveal your inmost secrets to a strange man. When you have to shout them it is even more difficult. So he and I did not exactly relate well to each other.

Finally he said, "Tell me about your dreams." So I scanned back in time for something really interesting that might impress him. "Well, the other night I dreamed about a boa constrictor," I said, starting at the top of my list of nocturnal imageries. He did not let me finish. He'd heard all he needed. "Get married, young lady," he said. "Anybody can get married if she makes the effort. Go out and get yourself a husband." And our interview was over.

Since it was wartime and I was in a big, strange city, there was little to be done about his suggestion; so the whole interview was a fizzle as far as I was concerned. Several years later, when I was in Daytona Beach, I told my friend Wally about my episode with the psychiatrist who wore a hearing aid and didn't seem to like my dream about a boa constrictor. Wally shrieked with laughter and pointed out that my analyst had obviously been Freudian. "You know what Freud says about snakes," Wally said. Then I recalled that they, as well as almost everything else, were phallic symbols to Freud. "And you not only told of dreaming about snakes, but a boa constrictor at that!" Wally whooped some more.

Not being impressed by Freud's belief that almost anything is a sex symbol, I have a much more intelligent explanation for the poor old boa. He must have been trying to reveal to me how my life was constricted by that job and how I was being crushed by my environment . . . and my loneliness.

Toward the end of that year as a hospital secretary, I was so completely miserable that I tried to kill myself. One who has so much resilience and resistance to life's pressures would have to be pushed by numerous agonies before such a final decision as this could be made. The reasons causing anyone to attempt to kill himself are intensely personal and difficult to bring to the light of public scrutiny. They are inevitably highly complex and involve an accumulation of depressing events. Over a time, many worries must pile up in the mind until there comes such a feeling of helplessness that there is an inability to endure another moment of life. In Baltimore I had an aggregation of negative emotions that became just too much for me. It was the loneliness, aggravated by my physical suffering, however, that finally did me in.

I went to my doctor one rainy afternoon for something to relieve the more or less constant arthritic pain the streptococcal septicemia had left me with. When he could suggest nothing more helpful than aspirin, something in me rebelled completely. I just was not going through life hurting most of the time (or so I thought then). I asked the doctor for some sleeping pills, and sensing my latent hysteria, he wisely prescribed a liquid medication.

Clutching the bottle like an amulet in my hand all the way

home, I tried to find any possible reason for not imbibing its entire contents. But I could not. So, on my return to my room, I sat down at my desk and composed a letter: "Mother, dearest, forgive me for what I am doing. Life is just too unbearable. . . ."

Now that I was entirely resolved, I eagerly began swallowing the medicine. The bottle's contents could not be drunk straight down, for it would have come straight up, so I took the potion spoonful by spoonful, secure in the belief that if I got down enough of it, oblivion forever would result. But with each sip I became more and more nauseated, and finally it was impossible to lift the spoon to my mouth once more. I barely made it to my bed to rest a few moments until the malaise might pass and my deadly chore be continued.

The birds were chirping merrily when I awoke to a sunny morning, and I never felt better in my life. I joined them in song, actually dancing around the room in happiness to find myself alive and greeted by such a beautiful day.

Happiness always comes after a stretch of misery like that . . . if you live through it. I realize that, as much as anything, my character has been built by a series of minor hard knocks and loneliness. Turning those stumbling blocks into stepping stones was next to impossible without the help of the Lord. As mentioned earlier, He was always guiding my footsteps, one way or another, without my knowing it; that is obvious now. But it was only when I became aware of this that I really began to sparkle inwardly.

CHAPTER X

"Call to Me, and
I Will Answer You"*

I set out on a lecture tour during the summer of 1975 with
mixed emotions. I would be speaking at a variety of psychic
centers in the East and the Midwest, especially a number of
Spiritual Frontiers Fellowship chapters. I did not know just
how I would be able to interrelate my talks on my psychic past
with my new religious experience, but I knew it had to be
done. So during each talk I made some comment about my
revelation, saying that I would go into more detail about it during the questions-and-answers period if anyone wanted to hear
it. Invariably there was a question that let me go into it, and
much interest in what was said about it. These people are
seekers, and many of them do not think they have found the
final answer. In fact, it seems to me that many seekers in the
psychic and occult fields are better prospects for the Baptism in
the Holy Spirit than your average sinner.

Many readers of my books write or telephone me from all
over the country when they have unpleasant or violent incidents of apparent possession or obsession by evil spirits. Previously I could only tell them to surround themselves with the
white Christ light and to affirm, "Nothing can come near me
or in any way affect me that does not come from God in love

* Jer. 33:3 (New American Bible)

and peace." Now I can advise them also to renounce the intruder and demand in the name of Jesus Christ that it leave—and they have better and quicker results. I suggest Pentecostal services, where they will find ministers who will cast out their demons. They can also get assistance at meetings of the Full Gospel Business Men's Fellowship International. The businessmen are great ones for chasing the devil.

I have bought copies of Sherrill's and Merlin Crothers' and Corrie Ten Boom's and others' books and passed them out to my friends, and several are now interested in trying to attain what I have found. I really have discovered myself actually proselytizing for the Lord. In my work in the psychic field, I presented facts as I saw them but made no effort to convert anyone to my beliefs. Now I am eager to share what I have with everyone who can safely be talked to about it. And I have placed myself completely in God's hands, and He is taking care of me as He has never done before.

I find myself particularly able to talk to skeptics and those in the psychic field who are still searching, for I am not yet so doctrinal in my approach as to think that my interpretation of Scripture or anything else is the only interpretation. My friend author Martin Ebon wrote to me about this (and I love him for it): "I am taking your involvement in the charismatic movement with the greatest seriousness and respect—particularly as your own detachment, sense of humor and sense of wonder make you an especially persuasive New Believer." A quotable quote if there ever was one.

I have attended a number of other charismatic retreats at Picture Rocks. One was held by Father Dick Schiblin on January 16–18, 1976, and it was another heart-warming and invigorating experience. We were asked during a workshop to write "What I Believe," and it was evident that my thoughts had changed considerably since my first retreat:

> I believe in a loving father God, in Jesus Christ,
> and in the Holy Spirit, and I believe they are all one
> as the great spiritual light and love of the universe.

Jesus is the beautiful life that revealed to us that we are not separate from God but one with Him, and that we will live forever. It is necessary for us to be aware of this, and Jesus is the key through which we can be. When we praise the Lord and praise Jesus, we are linking ourselves to the great God force—we are opening the door of knowledge of our oneness with God and our receptivity to His all-abiding, constant love. This feeling of contact is the presence of the Holy Spirit within us. It is God and Jesus in action.

During the whole of 1975 and the first half of 1976, I kept in mind the prophecy about me that had come at my first retreat and tried to think how I could be of use to Jesus in the way of writing a book about the Christian religion. Once, on the "700 Club" television program, Ben Kinchlow, the handsome black man who assists handsome Pat Robertson, made a statement that seemed to apply to me. A singer was telling him that she wanted to be of service to God, but she was not sure just how. Ben said, "Perhaps sometimes you ask God to use you and expect Him to make a beautiful silver gravy ladle of you; but he may instead need a big old coffee mug, and he uses you for that."

I wanted to be sure not to try to make a silver gravy ladle out of myself for the Lord if He could use me better in some other way. I've always been more the coffee-mug type, anyway.

There was no idea in my mind what kind of book to write or how to go about starting it. But I was willing to make the attempt. Dr. Robert Schuller spoke in his televised "Hour of Power" sermon one Sunday about people who hesitate to make commitments until they are sure they can succeed. Well, I'm not that kind of person. Having made my commitment to the Lord, I would start to write His book even without knowing how to go about it, and I became more and more eager to get to work. I hoped for inspiration to know what to do and when, but had no idea how it might come.

In my prayers, I often asked what the Lord wanted to do with me; and on Monday night of the last week in April—just a year from the time I received the Baptism—I asked again. Lying in bed preparing for my prayers, I was thinking about how He might talk to one, as so many have said He does. Does He use a "still, small voice" down inside you? Or is it what might be called "independent voice," in the room completely outside of one's person?

At the time I was pondering these things, I had not yet heard adorable, pixie-faced Dr. Schuller's "Hour of Power" sermon in which he talked about "How Two-Way Prayer Really Works." If so, I might have felt more secure about what was to happen to me this night. Dr. Schuller mentioned the passage in Jeremiah (33:3, *Revised Standard Version*) that reads, "Call to me and I will answer you, and will tell you great and hidden things which you have not known." He also quoted Dr. Viktor Frankl's book *The Unconscious God*, in which he psychoanalyzes the conscience.

Frankl says: "Conscience is not only a fact within psychological eminence, but a reference to transcendence. Only with reference to transcendence can it be understood." Dr. Schuller then said, "In two-way prayer you ask questions: 'Lord, am I moving in the right direction?' And you hear the voice say, 'Yes' or 'No.' You may think you are talking to yourself, but you're not. That's one of the exciting things that Viktor Frankl says in his book. He says, in effect, unless you are aware of the fact that the conscience is a transcendence that results from your original divine heritage, you will think that you are only talking to yourself. But in fact you are not talking to yourself. It is God speaking to you."

Even though I did receive confirmation of my experience from the Bible, it is consoling to realize that not only an eminent minister but an eminent psychiatrist as well can confirm its reality. For, that night, I had begun talking to God about what to write that would be of value to Him. Soon I was soaring with delight when praying in tongues. I had no idea whether or not what was spoken was a real language. It might have been Hebrew or Aramaic, or then again, it might have been gibberish. But it was a therapeutic release and a beautiful experience, as always. Then I stopped, said, "Praise You, Lord, and thank You," and thought my prayers were finished. But I spoke again briefly in tongues, and after that it was interpreted orally. What came out of my mouth were these words: "This is Jesus. I will make you my amanuensis. You will write a book that I want written."

He said a bit more, the details of which I have forgotten, and then paused. Then I spoke aloud on my own, saying, "Lord, please pardon my reluctance to believe you. I love you and want to talk to you and to do a book for you. But there are so many crackpots who sit around receiving alleged communications from Jesus that are pure drivel, or mostly commonplace platitudes, so I am necessarily very wary of this. Also, as you surely know, I am aware from personal experience that mischievous or malevolent spirits can talk to me and claim to be important personages, or my mother, or anyone else I want."

A few more words were spoken in the unknown language in answer to this, and then the translation was given: "You can tell it is I and not some intruder by the great joy you feel."

I had no argument for that. My heart was pounding ecstatically. So I took Him at His own evaluation and asked for some advice. I had been planning to have surgery in June to have a new hip socket implanted on my left side, and I was beginning to fear it. He replied that I should go ahead with the operation, that I would have loving protection, and that it would be successful.

Then he called me by name, saying, "Susy, I want you to learn to use the Bible so that I can talk to you with it."

I had been unsuccessful at letting the Bible drop open randomly and finding, as many people do, a message that exactly fits the situation in question. When I did that, it usually opened to the "begats" or to some talk about slaying your enemy, and this turns me off. But now, being urged to try to learn this technique, I agreed. There were a few more words of commendation and encouragement, and that was the end of my wonderful conversation.

I lay in bed after that and told myself not to take it too seriously. I had been fooled so many times before, and especially just recently with Mother and James. If Jesus wanted to convince me, He could just show Himself to me as He has to so many others. I then recalled a brief dream sequence a month prior to this, when, as I awoke, someone in a white robe was in the air obliquely above me with arms outstretched in benediction. This had set me up considerably; but I did not see a face, and it was so fleeting that it was hard to be sure who it might be. I hoped it was Jesus but was willing to settle for an angel. Now I thought about this, wondered about the reality of the whole conversation, and went to sleep in great happiness.

The next morning, my jubilation was quite restrained, as I told myself it could so easily have been some intruding spirit "putting me on." I sat down to my brief religious meditation thoroughly controlled emotionally. Still, it might not hurt to try what He had said about getting a message from my Bible. I picked it up and let it fall open on my lap, then glanced down at the top left corner of the page. It was John 10:1–5. (New American Bible):

"Truly I assure you:
Whoever does not enter the sheepfold through the gate
     but climbs in some other way
     is a thief and a marauder.
The one who enters through the gate is shepherd of the
   sheep;
     the keeper opens the gate for him.
The sheep hear his voice
     as he calls his own by name
     and leads them out.
When he has brought out all those that are his,
     he walks in front of them,
     and the sheep follow him
     because they recognize his voice.
They will not follow a stranger;
     such a one they will flee,
     because they do not recognize a stranger's voice."

After that, I thought frequently about the book for Jesus. I did not want to rush it, for I must be sure, every step of the way, to be following His dictates—if He did me the honor to carry on with this. I finally started it before going to the hospital, and worked on it all summer and fall while convalescing, writing it prayerfully, with love and joy in my heart.

CHAPTER XI

"...It Is He That Talketh with Thee"*

It is so easy to mislead yourself with wishful thinking and a desire to be cherished by someone great and wonderful, and most especially by your Lord. Certainly many people who believe themselves to be receiving scripts from Jesus are only self-deluded. So, perhaps, are some who believe He talks to them in their minds. In a few instances, this has occurred to me in a way that makes me feel fairly confident about it. Once, it was quite humorous.

One day, during my prayers, there must somehow have flashed across my mind something about how alone I am in the world and what a long, uphill journey it has been to try to develop my character. Possibly I felt a bit smug about how much had been accomplished, although I don't recall the details of it. Anyway, I mentally received this brief message: "I am proud that you built your character on your own, but more proud that you realize with me how much farther you have to go." This was a backhanded compliment if I ever received one, and *very* funny to me. I have always maintained that the Lord has to have a fantastic sense of humor, and now this was proof to me.

On the whole, however, in order to feel secure that I am

* John 9:37 (King James)

truly in touch with my Heavenly Source, I check important things with the Bible as He told me to in tongues. In my prayers at night, I ask a question or present a problem, and the next morning during my Scripture reading I let the Bible fall open for an answer. I have been so delighted to have that marvelous experience of having the answer fit the question exactly!

Here are a few instances of how confirmation has been received from my Bible:

The meditation group that had been meeting at my home had gradually been changing into a prayer meeting of sorts, and we had decided to undertake a study of the Bible. On the night of April 29, 1976, we read aloud parts of the Book of Revelation and discussed the meaning of the passages. We had a hard time making sense of it. I especially found it difficult and said so. "I have known many people who have visions and dreams that can be interpreted as something special," I said, "and most of them make a lot more sense than this does."

The next morning, after my prayers, I said aloud, "Lord, I just don't understand Revelation. Why do we have to try to make sense out of it?" Then I laid my Bible on my lap and let it drop open to get a message. What my eyes fell on was Luke 24, Verses 36 through 45: "While they were still speaking about all this, he himself stood in their midst and said to them, 'Peace to you.' . . . Then he opened their minds to the understanding of the Scriptures." (New American Bible)

As time goes on, this understanding is beginning to come to me, along with enjoyment in reading the Bible.

Over the Memorial Day weekend I drove to the scenic Oak Creek Canyon with the Harrisons in their Winnebago motor home. During the trip, Mary read from the Bible a verse from Isaiah that spoke of God telling the Hebrews to slay their enemies. I became very intense about this, saying that the God I could understand would not encourage wars and certainly would not tell His people to go out and slay others. "When the God of the Old Testament is depicted as vengeful, I cannot understand or accept Him as my kind of God," I said vehemently.

The next morning, this was still on my mind during my prayers. I spoke to God, telling Him frankly my feelings about it. Then I turned to the Bible for a message, and my eyes fell on John 17:25–26: "Just Father, the world has not known you, but I have known you; and these men have known that you sent me. To them I have revealed your name, and I will continue to reveal it so that your love for me may live in them, and I may live in them." (New American Bible)

To me, this says that the God Jesus knew was not the God that the world knew. Although Jesus spoke of Him as a strict judge, not a fond and indulgent parent, still he was a Father, and a *just* Father. Paul describes "the God of our Lord Jesus Christ" as a "glorious Father." (Ephesians 1:17, Good News)

On June 17, prior to going into the hospital to have the hip socket implant replacing my weak left hip, primarily so that I could walk with more strength and take the weight off my arthritic knees, I began to get cold feet (figuratively, not literally). Friends were pointing out the severity of the operation and its possible dangers, and I was almost becoming afraid to go through with it. So I prayed about it, asking if I really should have it done. Then I turned to the New American Bible for a message. It fell open at Hebrews 12:12: "So strengthen your drooping hands and your weak knees. Make straight the paths you walk on, that your halting limbs may not be dislocated but healed."

Even with this reassurance, I prayed about it again time after time: "Oh, Lord, please be with me through my surgery and make everything successful." On the morning of the 22nd, just the day before the operation, I opened my Bible for an encouraging answer. It turned to Revelation 2:10: "Do not be afraid of anything you are about to suffer." (Good News) You see, already I was learning to appreciate Revelation.

By September 17 the manuscript of this book was in proper order and just barely acceptable to me. But was it acceptable to my Heavenly Source? I was not sure whether or not some material had been included that should not be in it and some left out that should. Not feeling comfortable about it at this point,

I decided to ask in my prayers for an evaluation, and then
turned to the Bible for my answer. It opened at Ecclesiastes,
Chapter 8, and as I read along, about the wise man and the king,
at first there did not seem to be anything that fitted my needs.
I began to suspect that, this once, Scripture had failed me with
an answer. Then I came to Verse 6: ". . . for there is a time
and a judgment for everything." (New American Bible) That
was my perfect answer, and I realized that at the right time my
evaluation would be forthcoming.

Some friends who are old hands at reading the Bible mentioned to me that many people do what I am doing and get answers from their Bibles—as if I didn't know it. They also said
that when you went to your Bible for an answer it frequently
was not there—you couldn't find a thing on the page that was
applicable to your situation. This I also knew, because that had
always been my problem before I began to get my prayer messages. There must be a mandate before my specific answer will
be in my Bible.

There was a time after I had finished the first draft of this
manuscript and sent it to the publisher that I tried for contact
nonetheless. I did not feel like asking for further comment
from my Heavenly Source, since He had said it was not the
time for judgment; but I kept letting my Bible fall open anyway, just in case there might be some kind of heartening word.
Since I really knew the manuscript was not yet good enough
for praise, I went at this without enthusiasm. And there was
never anything that could apply to my situation on the pages
that turned open on those occasions.

When I finally heard from my editor about the book, he
suggested so much change that I felt swamped at first. That
night, I went into prayer for encouragement and requested a
definite message. The next morning, my Bible opened immediately to Psalm 69, titled "A Cry for Help." Instead of reading
it, however, my eyes fell on the line just above it, at the end of
Psalm 68: "He gives strength and power to his people. Praise
God!" (Good News) So I did praise Him, knowing the

strength and power to revise the manuscript would be forth-coming.

I began immediately to look over the editor's suggestions and felt considerably encouraged that night when I prayed again. The next morning, I turned to the Bible not for a new message but to find the uplifting lines of the day before. My bookmark, which pinches a clip of pages, opened this time at the back of the clip. It was Psalm 77: "I cry aloud to God; I cry aloud, and he hears me." (Good News) So I got two for the price of one on that occasion.

On January 10, 1977, just before sending this manuscript to the publisher for the second time, I prayed for a further message about it. Once again, I was hoping for some kind of "Well done." What was received instead was Acts 1:8, where Jesus Himself says, ". . . and you will be witness for me in Jerusalem, in all of Judea and Samaria, and to the ends of the earth." (Good News) One could not ask for a better send-off for a book than that, so happiness about this statement has been growing and growing in my heart ever since.

I do not mean to suggest that such things as this happen only to me. It is one of the continuing miracles of Christianity that such blessings are probably daily occurrences for countless people.

Christian Broadcasting Network president Pat Robertson tells in *The Flame*, December 1976, about signing a contract on December 31, 1975, to purchase a 142-acre site in Virginia Beach on which to build the CBN International Communications Center, which will house a satellite earth station to preach Christ's message to the entire world. On New Year's Day 1976, as Pat prayed for a special word from the Lord, his eyes fell on Jeremiah 1:10 (Living Bible): "Today your work begins, to warn the nations and the kingdoms of the world."

CHAPTER XII

"The Will of the
Lord Be Done"*

Except when I pray and then go to the Bible for an answer, I
have learned not to push for my guidance, for it will come
when least expected. An interesting indication of this occurred
on the night of November 12, 1976, during a time that the
book had been put aside for a few days to let it simmer, as I
did not know just how to handle certain aspects of it. I had a
dream in which a statement about Jesus was going over and
over in my mind. Awakening from it, I wrote on my bedside
note pad: "Jesus knew His time had come because nothing
went right for Him. If God had not been ready for His Son to
return to Him, there would have been no way that He could
have been crucified. Events, instead, would have exonerated
Him completely."

As I lay there thinking about that statement and wondering
why it had been given, the realization came that my own life
has revealed many situations that went smoothly because it was
the will of God, and others that were a big fiasco because it was
not right for me to have gotten myself into them. The Lord
knows the tenor our lives should take and what experiences will
best forward our growth. When it is right with Him for them
to occur, then everything falls into place. When it is not right,

* Acts 21:14 (King James)

then it seems that nothing we can do will improve the situation until we just remove ourselves from it.

Throughout my lifetime, I have always seemed to be in the wrong situation on every possible occasion. Why would I get into trouble or have things go wrong when others could go through the same incidents with no problems whatever? Most likely, it was because I was determined to have my own way, not because of being a selfish only child who wanted things for myself, but because I had high standards of what was right and wrong for any given situation and thought deliberate action on my part could change it for the better. If events were not going as it seemed that they should, I did everything possible to alter them, usually causing havoc.

It is sad to see so many people like me working so hard to cause things to happen the way they think they should and then usually finding the results ineffective or even downright harmful. "Let go and let God" is a phrase one often hears in metaphysical circles, and it is also used in Christian churches and fellowships as well. I learned this phrase during the days of my psychical research but never really began to apply it in my life until after I had the Baptism in the Holy Spirit. Now, in my present stage of knowledge, I turn everything over to Jesus and the Holy Spirit, and all goes well.

Jesus was always calm and receptive to the inspiration of His Father in Heaven. In order for us to lead successful lives, we have to be also. In the end, we invariably have to surrender and relax and let divine ideas flow into us. Why not do it in the first place? Instead, we try to fight our way through any and every situation without initially asking what is the Lord's will. Most of us get swamped with trouble before we finally learn to let God rule our lives.

A brief flashback revealing this covers the time I tried to live in Mexico. It came indirectly out of my investigation of witchcraft, and perhaps that is why nothing went smoothly from the beginning—because it was involved, however innocently, with something evil.

I had never wanted to do a book on witchcraft, but Prentice-

Hall and my agent got together to convince me I should write *Today's Witches*. Since it was to be an appraisal or survey of the current situation, not a paean of praise, I finally agreed. In it I did not say anything too pleasant about witches. In fact, I understand the witches of this country who became aware of its existence were quite upset. Some of them may even have put me on their hex list. I know that the book never did sell—bombed, as they say in the trade—and that could have been the reason. It was certainly as well done and as interesting as I could make it.

While I said nothing favorable about witchcraft, it was necessary to admit that some witches have power and should not be taken lightly. It was rather disquieting to write some of the tales about things they have done. I learned that even white witches, who purport to produce only good manifestations, know how to perform evil acts if they want to. A famous one said exactly that on the Virginia Graham television show one day. Virginia asked, "What is the difference between black witches and white witches?" She was told something to the effect that black witches perform bad acts, while white witches do good. However, a white witch knows all the tricks, and if someone does something to her she does not like, it is easy enough for her to zap him (or her).

I think it is especially unfortunate that so many young people have taken up witchcraft lately. In fact, now it is said to be not so much the interest of the college set as of high school kids. It is to be hoped it is just a passing fad.

I spent three days in Toronto in 1968 investigating a group of hippie witches. They took me to some of their coven meetings in the Yorkville Strip, the hippie hangout, and told me many stories of their experiences. I like being with young people, but it made me very, very sad to see this group in the condition they were in. I wrote about them in *Today's Witches*: ". . . the experience impressed me because it gave me the opportunity to associate closely with the typical life of the hippie in a commune. These were sweet kids, and apparently harmless . . . except to themselves. But they were in a terribly sad state because they were all high on drugs of one kind or another. If nothing else, it robbed them of their youth. Young people should have pep and vigor and enthusiasm. These just sat around on the floor, leaning their backs against the walls or the furniture, and stared into space."

The witchcraft they performed was very feeble, as can be imagined. However, the tales they had to tell of their experiences and those of other witch acquaintences were phenomenal. I did not know how much to believe, and yet some of it was bound to be true. I was rather glad to escape from this environment when time came to leave.

Before *Today's Witches* was finished, I signed a contract with World Publishing Company for a sequel to *Prominent American Ghosts*. It was to be titled *Ghosts Around the House*. I had been invited to lecture to the San Antonio chapter of Theta Sigma Phi, the newspaperwomen's honorary sorority, at their installation ceremonies in March. So I arranged a tour around the Midwest and the South to gather material for the new book while on my way to Texas. The luncheon meeting at which I spoke was held in the new Hilton Hotel in La Villita, the recently remodeled old Mexican quarter in San Antonio, and I was made an "honorary mayor" of La Villita. The newspaper publisher who sat next to me and introduced me at the luncheon could not talk enough about San Miguel de Allende, Cuernavaca, Taxco, and other beautiful Mexican cities, as ideal for Americans. He said it was much less expensive and altogether charming to live there. And he sold me on the idea of moving to Mexico. I thought it would be wise to preview it first, however.

It was easy to decide that some chapters on Mexico were necessary for my witch book, for witchcraft is completely accepted among most of the primitive natives—and recognized for what it is worth by the more sophisticated. I had been corresponding with several people there who had read my books, and one of them, an American expatriate whom I will call Robin Robinson, asked me to visit his wife and him in Cuernavaca.

I accepted their invitation, and in early August away I flew.

Not on a broomstick, as a proper witchcraft researcher should travel, but by Aeronaves de México. Handsome young Robin and his pretty wife, Elaine, met me at the airport in Mexico City and took me to their apartment in Cuernavaca, where I spent several pleasant weeks. Then I stayed a few days at a hotel in Mexico City, then lectured at a luncheon meeting of the American Club. After that I was a house guest of the young manager of the club and his wife for two weeks. This girl was a great help to me in researching witchcraft there, and we visited the charming native markets and other areas of interest. Then I flew home by way of Yucatán, where I satisfied a life-long ambition to visit the fascinating Mayan ruins at Chichén Itzá.

I learned on this trip that my limited college Spanish was usable for travel communication. But the Lord knew it would not be sufficient for living south of the border. I am sure he tried to give me many hints that the time was not ripe for me to settle in a foreign country, but I ignored them all. Back in Miami, I could think of little else but returning to flowering, friendly Mexico. When Robin and Elaine phoned that they had found a large house in an American compound we could all share, it sounded delightful, and I bent every effort to get there as quickly as possible. *Today's Witches* was finished in short order and sent to the publisher. Then I began selling all my furniture and other possessions—every object that would not fit into or on top of my car.

Everything went wrong or was as complicated as possible. This should have been an indication to me that this was not God's will (or what was best for me), but I would not have believed it then. Although there was a sublease clause in my contract for my apartment, the owner never gave back my deposit of a month's rent, even though I finally procured a renter to take my place. I left all my valuable psychic books—some twenty-five or so cartons—with a man who claimed to be a friend; but when I finally asked for them back several years later, he returned only seven cartons of mostly old magazines and denied having any more.

Several people from time to time planned to accompany me on the trip to help with the driving, and one by one they backed out for some reason. So my companion was finally a Fort Lauderdale woman I had met in the hotel in Mexico City who wanted to return. Although she had promised to help with the driving, she would never take the wheel unless conditions were prime and pleasant, so it turned out I did most of the driving myself. She also proved to be the world's worst sport in every other way, screaming and hollering if everything did not go exactly as she wanted.

I was driving—and still am, for that matter—a 1962 Cadillac Coupe de Ville that I had bought secondhand; and there were some unpleasant adventures with it along the way. First, in Tallahassee I asked a service-station attendant to check the water, but not liking to become involved with all that steam, he evidently did not do it. Later, along a highway with few exits, smoke began pouring from the engine of the car. After a lot of worry, we eventually got off and to a garage in a minute village, where we had to remain overnight while a new water pump was installed—at a cost of seventy-five dollars.

When one crosses into Mexico, he has to tip the border guards; and because my car was packed to the brim and had a carrying rack on top that was also piled high, we were excellent game for them. One threatened to make me take everything out of the trunk, and so I gave him a tip to quiet his demands. He brought up a friend who threatened to make me take everything out of the tonneau and off the top—until he was tipped. A third guard arrived. Same threats. Same gratuities. It cost me seventeen dollars to cross the border.

By then, it was four in the afternoon, and we hoped to make Monterrey our stop for the evening. There was so much road repair, or lack of it, going on in Reynosa, the border city, that most of the streets to be traversed had deep ruts. We did not know it then, but the bumpy roads jarred some wires loose in the car's lighting system.

Being late in starting, we hoped to stop for the night somewhere en route to Monterrey, not realizing that we would never once see the lights of a town along the entire stretch. When we still had about one hundred miles to go, it became dark enough to turn on the lights, and we *had* none. I fooled with the lighting levers and eventually discovered that if my foot was kept on the distance button, one parking light could be held on. And thus I drove all the way to Monterrey, with my left foot awkwardly and uncomfortably stretched over to the light button.

My companion was appalled that anyone would attempt to drive across a barren stretch in the Mexican night with a car whose lights were not functioning properly, although what she had to offer in exchange could not be learned. She also had unkind things to say about a person who would start out from Miami in a car that was going to fall apart on the trip. Although it did not seem amusing at the time, I can't help but recall with a mean little grin what happened next. As we drove along, she kept saying over and over again, "I'm going to have a nervous breakdown. I'm going to have a nervous breakdown. I'm going to scream! I'm going to scream!" Now, trying to follow my mother's teachings, I had become a pretty patient lady, but finally, after about an hour of this, I had heard it once too often. I pulled over to the side of the barren highway, stopped the car, and said, "Be my guest. Please yell all you wish right now and get it over with. Then I don't want to hear another word out of you." She didn't scream; but she did hush up after that.

It was a fairly exhausted Susy who pulled into Monterrey about eight-thirty or nine o'clock. We spent the night in the first sleazy hotel we came to, had the car repaired the next morning, and proceeded along our way with no more trouble until we arrived in Cuernavaca and my passenger was unloaded, with much relief on my part.

It was necessary to go to the police station to ask for directions to the compound where Robin and Elaine had rented a house for us, because they were not home to answer the telephone and no one could understand my queries for directions. Two police officers guided me there, one, who knew the way, in his car in front, the other in my car interpreting his signals for me. I did not know it then, but they should have been tipped handsomely for this service when they finally brought me to the gate, rang the bell, and explained to the porter who I was. I did thank them profusely, and, although that was not what they had in mind, they accepted smiles instead of tips.

The house to be shared with the Robinsons was beautiful, but I soon began to realize it was not for me. Living with a strange young couple did not prove easy, and finally Robin gave me an excuse to leave. I had learned that he was a boozer, and one day he became very upset about some slight in a letter from his sister. By evening he had convinced himself of the necessity to drown himself in a bottle in order to assuage his hurt feelings. I went to bed about eleven in my suite of rooms, which was in an ell to the main house, adjoining the kitchen wall; but I could not sleep because Robin sat in the kitchen noisily imbibing, singing, and talking to himself. I heard Elaine tell him good night, and then for an hour he remained alone and practiced karate or kung-fu or whatever it was. He loudly proclaimed all kinds of guttural noises that sounded like ki-ai, and hic and haec and hoc, as he struck the walls with his fists or his feet.

Much later, I heard him go to his room, and then Elaine screamed, "Oh, *no*, Robin, *don't!*" No further sound was heard from them the rest of the night, but I did not sleep so well. By nine in the morning, when Elaine usually appeared, there was not the teensiest sound to be heard from them. By ten, nothing. Eleven, no Elaine. Twelve, when Robin usually arose, no Robin and no Elaine. By then, I was visualizing a scene of mayhem in their room, sure that the drunken Robin must have killed his wife with a karate chop and then passed out. I actually was trembling with anticipation of something I did not want to know, when at one o'clock the two of them appeared as fresh and crisp and innocent as white daisies.

That was the day I told them it would be best for us to part, since I was not quite up to living with modern youths whose ways were so divergent from my own. A real-estate agent found me a nice suite of rooms in a modern house with a middle-aged

Mexican couple who spoke English, and I settled down more comfortably. But I was lonely every minute of those days and nights.

The climate in Cuernavaca was miraculous all winter. I had never felt better in years. The beauty of the city thrilled me, for it has many hills and barrancas (ravines) covered with assorted quaint old buildings, shacks, and modern palaces. The homes of Cuernavaca's wealthy are hidden behind walls over which creep flowering vines, especially the purples and reds of bougainvillaea. In the early spring the trees bloom, their bouquets of flowers peeping over all the walls and dotting the hills and valleys with color, the lavender jacarandas being particularly magnificent. In the distance, on clear days, could be seen the snow-covered peaks of the twins, Popocatépetl and Ixtacihuatl.

In spite of all this, I never learned to feel at home in Mexico. It was mostly the language barrier that caused this, and others have since told me that they have had the same problem. My best efforts and all the studying I did there still produced only what is known as kitchen Spanish. I knew enough to communicate my wishes to the numerous pretty little housemaids, and usually to the shopkeepers. But an intelligent conversation with educated Mexicans, whose English was usually as poor as my Spanish, was impossible. And so we made little pleasantries at one another, both of us sounding fairly feeble-minded. You cannot work up much rapport in this manner, although the Mexican people are so gracious and sweet you really want to get to know them better.

Well, numerous other things went wrong, for it was obviously not right for me to be there; and so, for many good reasons, I exited Mexico in late March. I left part of my heart there, but I will have to have the Lord's permission before ever trying to spend any length of time there again. The moment I decided to leave, everything fell into place, and the trip home, in good company, was uneventful. At the time, I did not learn my lesson from this experience, but looking back at it now, I can see how necessary it is to take God's highway as we chug along through life.

CHAPTER XIII

"...Try the Spirits Whether They Are of God"*

When we find things going wrong with everything we try to do, we should know then that we are not following God's will. Sometimes, however, when things go completely haywire it may be more than just an individual's willfulness involved. It may be the influence of evil spirits instead. I feel it important to advise of the possibility of this, since some weak persons get into such situations unwittingly. There were several instances I came upon in my studies that brought home to me clearly how spirits of the dead can influence an individual negatively and cause great harm.

Of course, for all those who have frightening experiences caused by their efforts at automatic writing and such, there are others who receive at least something of value, as I eventually did. But most acquire a great amount of drivel claiming to be from pompous master teachers, angelic spirits, or even Jesus Himself. One can become so entranced by such grandiloquent messages that his ego may expand beyond normal limits. I know many who believe all the material they receive to be gospel and give it no critical evaluation whatsoever. And I must admit that although I made every effort to keep my feet on the ground over the information received from my mother and

* I John 4:1 (King James)

from James, it was difficult at times not to think of it as the ultimate authority.

Unfortunately, many who are neurotic or even possibly psychotic find the trappings of the whole occult bag immensely appealing. Often those with tensions, anxieties, and fears, who can be the most susceptible to obsession or possession, are highly attracted to all the wrong aspects of the field. They are the ones who try to use telepathy to influence the mind of another, who become involved in witchcraft, who take up magical rituals, or who hold weird and eerie séances. And they invite whatever trouble they get.

Although I personally believe from the evidence of my own experience that these mental intrusions are by the spirits of evil men or juvenile delinquents who once lived on earth, I cannot claim for certain that demons are not acting instead, in the name of spirits of the dead. If you want to say it is the Devil doing it, go ahead. I am not going to fight anyone on this point. I only know that I John 4:1 says, "Beloved, believe not every spirit, but try the spirits whether they are of God. . . ." (King James) Or, as the New American Bible reads: "Beloved, / do not trust every spirit, / but put the spirits to a test / to see if they belong to God, / because many false prophets have appeared in the world." To me this says that John knew of the existence of spirits and that some were good and some were bad. Is there any other interpretation? The point is to *try* them, to *test* them, whatever they are, before you take the chance of getting involved with them.

Even if the Devil is not as rampant as some insist he is, certainly some evil force is, and it is not wise to encourage it by reaching out to spirits in such a way that you lay yourself open to their possibly negative influence. If someone you love has died, just send him loving thoughts and know that he is still cherishing you in return. You do not need to have him write, "This is Joe" or "Harry still loves you," to know that this is true.

I was told recently by my Heavenly Source: "*We do not want achievement in the psychic field,* and that is why there is so little success in communication." This was a revelation to me, and it helped me to understand the many failures in every kind of effort to prove the reality of life after death by scientific research. The information went on: "That is why people never get anywhere with it that is conclusive. We are so aware of the dangers of bad spirit influence that we do not want people to try to communicate even with good spirits. One is unaware whom he is communicating with, because he cannot see them, but they are most frequently evil or mischievous spirits. The time will come when people on earth will know for sure that they live after death, but continuous successful communication with spirits is a long time away."

Many people are going to continue to use the Ouija board, however, and this can be the opening wedge that allows an entity to take over a weak or neurotic person entirely. A friend of mine knew a woman who lost touch with reality completely over her alleged communication with spirits. She must have been emotionally unstable to begin with, and for some reason she believed every word that she received by automatic writing. At first her husband was also very interested, and for a while he encouraged her. But then he began to realize that she was becoming too receptive to it, even though obvious lies were sometimes written. Once, she made a long trip to visit relatives to verify something shocking that had been told her about a member of her family. It turned out to be untrue and she had made the whole trip for nothing.

Soon this woman was completely overpowered by the entity communicating through her. Her husband tried to locate a psychiatrist who could understand the possibility of a real possession case, but whatever treatment she had did nothing to help her. Shortly afterward, she tried to kill her husband with a butcher knife, and eventually she killed herself.

I knew a beautiful blonde in Miami, named Pearl, who suffered from being too sensitive psychically and not knowing how to control it. She was an alcoholic, and was grateful when it was suggested to her that the influence of evil or mischievous spirits of the dead was a large part of her problem. "I always wondered what kind of a devil could be hiding in my own subconscious mind," she told me. "It frightened me to death, for I seemed powerless to keep it from ruling my actions and causing me to drink. I thought I had a split personality and knew that if I went to a psychiatrist he might put me away, so I suffered with it alone."

Pearl began to realize that she was never alone, however. Inside her mind there was someone who spoke to her frequently, especially when she was out driving her car. She was so pretty that she always attracted men. Apparently she had also attracted some on the other side of the veil, for they talked to her in her mind, told her of their love for her, and invited her to join them in the spirit world. Once, as she was driving along, she was told, "You've got to come over here with me." Then the voice said, firmly and forcefully, "Kill yourself . . . right now! Drive into that tree." On this occasion Pearl managed to keep her senses and avoid doing what she was commanded to do. But unfortunately one night some months later, when she had been drinking, she was unable to resist. On the command "run into that telephone pole," she did. She totaled her car and did a good bit of damage to her jaw, necessitating many hours at the dentist and a great amount of money for the repairs to her teeth.

From my own observation, I am sure that it is possible for a person who has mental conflicts of one kind or another to be moved in on by an evil spirit and taken over completely. The disturbance known as poltergeist may be caused by such a situation. The case of the famous Miami poltergeist, in which I was personally involved, illustrates this point exactly.

A poltergeist is one of the weirdest manifestations of nature. Although quite rare, it still occurs frequently enough that most people will recall reading in their newspapers from time to time of rocks falling on an occasional besieged locale or dishes dashing about a house. I had heard and read about such goings on and knew they had occurred all through history, so I put as much credence in them as in any other well-attested phenomena. But there were reservations in my mind, because instinctively one does not accept the fact that inanimate objects can really fly through the air or fall from shelves when not propelled by some kind of human mechanisms.

Psychokinesis is the word used by parapsychologists to account for this unseemly activity. It is defined as an unusual and unknown force coming from the mind of a person who has a good deal of repressed emotion. There is always such an individual around somewhere when poltergeist activity is going on. Of course, the general public and most especially the press usually try to blame it on pranks and trickery by the person most closely involved. Spiritualists prefer to believe that mischievous spirits are causing the activity; and some Christians will most certainly see the hand of Satan in it. The poltergeist with which I became involved was definitely caused by some kind of devilish force, as the life of the youth under its influence was to continue to reveal for several years. From my observation of the boy during this time, I know the tragic consequences.

Even with my avidity for personal experience in all psychic areas, I hardly expected or even hoped that an opportunity would occur for me to see a genuine poltergeist in action. But on January 12, 1967, while living in Miami, I was being interviewed on a radio talk program and a woman called to say that glass beer mugs and dishes and boxes of all kinds were falling from the shelves of the warehouse where she worked; and nobody was there to push them. So naturally I rushed out to see what was going on. From the very beginning, boxes fell and dishes crashed from the shelves while I was there and able to observe that there was no one in any position to cause them to move by normal means.

It was soon to be revealed that most of the poltergeist activity, which had started suddenly, without warning, followed or was somehow centered around a handsome, likable nineteen-year-old Cuban refugee named Julio. It is obvious to me now that he had picked up one, or possibly more, malevolent entities who were to provide him excitement for a while, and do him great harm as time went on.

I soon called in eminent parapsychologists to investigate this case, and it has gone down in the records as one of the more interesting poltergeists, particularly of value because it was possible to put the involved youth under controlled conditions and still observe the violent supernormal activity going on around him.

My best proof of the reality of the manifestations occurred one noon when Julio and I were alone in the warehouse, for things fell under conditions just about as controlled as they are likely to get. Police officer David J. Sackett had decided to try an experiment and had wiped an amber glass beer mug clean of fingerprints and placed it as a decoy on the shelf on the far side of the fourth aisle in the warehouse. He then stretched a rope down the middle of aisle three and said that no one was to go on the other side of it past tier three into aisle four. Julio and I were outside this roped-off area, talking at the front desk in the warehouse, at twelve o'clock. I glanced around and realized that everyone else had gone to lunch and said, "There's nobody in here but us. Now's the time for something to happen."

At that very second we heard a pop and discovered that a shot glass had fallen into aisle three at the north end, just inside the rope. It was not broken. Without touching it, we left it there and returned to the desk, where I seated myself and began to write up the incident. Just then, a loud crash sounded from the same area. This time it was a beer mug, just outside the rope at the same end of the same aisle. It was thoroughly broken. Wondering if it might be the decoy mug that had been on the far side of this shelf, I crawled under the rope and checked to see if that was still in its original place and condition. It was. By the time I returned to Julio and the desk, a smashing retort reported that it was in aisle four in a thousand small pieces. And it was too far from the position it had had on the shelf to have just fallen off. It had had to fly some distance.

Since I had been talking to Julio and looking at him during every one of these events, I was certain he had not made any of them happen by conscious manipulation, trickery, or fraud.

After twenty-three days of more or less constant poltergeist activity, it was discovered that Julio had robbed the warehouse office the night before. He left so many stupid clues that it was impossible to suspect anyone else, and eventually he confessed. Of course he was fired, but the bad influence had not left him and it broke out in poltergeist activity at the next two places he worked. After he left a national chain shoe store in downtown Miami, I interviewed the manager and learned that for the two weeks Julio worked there many objects were displaced by supernormal means.

After Julio was fired from that job, he went to work in the Kress warehouse. While he was there, bottles of insecticides started exploding, then bottles of hand lotion and Vaseline. And brown shoe polish flew some forty feet. Then a shelf full of cups crashed. Much of this occurred while the young man was under observation, and the manager was sure he could not have done it himself by any kind of physical means. Julio resigned before he could be fired by Kress.

The youth's poltergeist did not limit itself to throwing things in the places where he worked. It caused him to perform ridiculous acts in his life experience as well. For instance, he went into a jewelry store to buy an engagement ring for his girl, María. As I understood it from him later, he signed up to make payments, giving his name and address, and then, without making a down payment, ran out of the store with the ring —right into the arms of a policeman. He spent some months in jail for that, but he did not learn from it. He actually seemed a bit proud of the attention his poltergeist brought him, so I doubt if he wanted to be rid of it at that point. Several exorcisms were performed by ministers who were sure the Devil had gotten hold of him, but the possessing entity retained its grip.

After he was released from prison, Julio and María were married, and the next year they had a baby girl. Shortly afterward, Julio was working at a service station alone one night when it was held up. Instead of giving up the money without a struggle, Julio told the man who asked for it at the point of a gun, "Try and get it." A shot was fired over his head.

Now, Julio is too smart a boy to do what he did next: he wrestled with the thief for the gun. It resulted in his being shot in the abdomen and his aorta being severed. He nearly died but was saved by a delicate operation. I visited him later in the hospital and learned that he was now frightened to death of his poltergeist and blamed it for his foolish acts. He was determined that it should have nothing further to do with his life.

I lost touch with Julio for several years, for I left Miami and he knew so little English that he was unable to write. In 1973 I received a Christmas card from him from a prison in Puerto Rico. He had been involved in armed robbery and incarcerated for a period of several years. While in jail, he had been studying English and had learned to write it quite well. He was also taking psychology courses and others, which had obviously improved his knowledge a great deal. Once again, he was swearing he would never do anything bad at any future date. He was sure he was no longer possessed.

I've heard from Julio several times since then. His term in the jailhouse is just about up and he will soon have a happy reunion with María and his little girl, who is now of school age. I can only wish them the very best.

CHAPTER XIV

"...Follow Not That
Which Is Evil..."*

It is not necessarily those who are attempting to communicate with spirits who get into trouble from them. Many good Christians may be more psychically sensitive than they realize and thus may not always be receiving from the Almighty when they think and hope they are. For this reason, those who believe they are having two-way conversations with God should be careful to evaluate what they receive to make sure it is always intelligent, loving, and sensible. And they should be aware of safeguards for protection, because the intrusions can occur *whether or not they believe in the possibility of such a thing.*

Although the illustrations I have to offer involve demented people who have undoubtedly become possessed by evil spirits or satanic influences, others, who are not at all deranged, may be self-deluded by their religious fervor and do things their intelligence should advise against, because they believe "God told me to do it" or "Jesus asked me."

Quite the most appalling thing I know about personally occurred to a Lutheran minister friend of mine (whom I shall call Ernest) on Thanksgiving Day, 1976. A tall, handsome man in his forties, Ernest had a Ph.D. from a southern university and had taught religion at the college level for some years. He

* III John 11 (King James)

also held clinics in Humanistic Psychology, and one of his patients was in much worse shape mentally than anyone realized. Ernest had written about him to a mutual friend of ours just two days before his death: "As long as I can keep one borderline psychotic from going off the deep end in Clinic, we should have a good holiday season." The patient, who was a charismatic, had several times told Ernest's wife how much he loved Ernest and appreciated the great help he was giving him.

On Thanksgiving morning Ernest was conducting a religious service in a new chapel he had recently built on his home property. His wife, who played the organ, his two daughters, and his mother-in-law were all present at the service, as well as the psychotic patient, his wife, and other friends and neighbors. While Ernest was praying, his eyes closed and his Bible in his hands, the patient pulled out a huge, sharp knife and slashed Ernest's throat, nearly decapitating him. Then, before anyone could stop him, he cut into Ernest's chest and thrust his hand in, attempting to pull out the heart. The most impossibly horrible thing about this was that all the time he was killing my friend, this man was shouting, "Praise the Lord" and "I'm doing this for Jesus."

An incident that closely involved me mentally with a crime occurred in the summer of 1966, when I was on my tour for *Prominent American Ghosts*. My friend Leah Exon (now Lusher) met me in Albany for the New England part of my tour. We went first to Kinderhook, New York, to investigate the home of President Martin Van Buren and its historical ghosts. Then we detoured over the Fourth of July weekend to visit Montreal, Quebec, and the Gaspé Peninsula. We came back into the States at Madawaska, at the topmost tip of Maine. This touring in Canada is detailed because it is important to the account that we had been away from American radio, television, and newspapers for several days. In the more remote areas of Quebec Province, we seldom heard anything but French spoken, and we had tried to reply in our own shaky French just to show how cosmopolitan we were.

On the Fourth of July itself we spent the day driving along

U.S. 1 in a very rural part of Maine, cruising through practically wild country with few habitations. It was pleasurable to amble along, stopping to eat the tiny, delectable wild strawberries that grew beside the road, or to look at anything that appealed to us. Once, we scared a bear cub away when we muscled in on his luscious lunch. Another time, a large stag with magnificent antlers loomed up ahead of us on the highway.

As we drove along, I told Leah of the ghost we would try to learn more about in Machiasport, Maine. Nelly Butler, the famous Machiasport ghost of 1799, was the first authentic, documented ghost in America. She had appeared to many people over a period of several months, and I hoped, even though it was almost two hundred years later, that she might make one last return engagement for our edification. Being still dumb about the nuances of protecting oneself, I sent out calls to her all during the day, asking her to show that night. She did not answer our invitation, but *someone* certainly did.

After dinner in Machias we returned to our quarters at the modern Bluebird Motel around ten o'clock, and I began to feel lightheaded the minute we entered the room—exactly as I had in London when I went into trance. I hastily prepared for bed, then hopped in, hoping that my condition might presage the appearance of Nelly Butler.

Leah was psychic too, but her reaction was a feeling of heaviness she did not like. She prayed aloud and asked that we be protected, no matter what might occur. After that, we waited quietly in the dimly lighted room.

Suddenly my head began to spin as if it were forcibly being pulled into a whirlpool. I felt myself losing consciousness and fought it, for it had never happened to me before and the idea was repulsive. Then, suddenly, I was chilled to the bone. My whole body was as cold inwardly and externally as if I'd been placed in a Deep-Freeze, and my stomach began to tremble with fright. Making a strong effort to regain control, I opened my eyes and sat up in bed, crying aloud, "No, this isn't right! I can't do it!"

Leah came over to me, eagerly agreeing with me. "I'm glad,"

she said. "I feel nervous about it, too. That's why I wanted the light on."

I was sure that something very evil was in the room, and it must have been trying to take me over. I told Leah that. Her response was emphatic: "It's obviously a bad influence of some kind. And I'm chilled to the bone."

I had not yet mentioned the extreme cold I had experienced, so it was obvious that it was external to me in the room. We were both badly frightened and began appealing for protection, and praying. Then Leah went back to bed and soon fell asleep. I was too nervous for that, and so watched the Johnny Carson show until it went off, at twelve-thirty. Then, leaving the lights on in both the alcove and the bathroom, I finally managed to get to sleep.

In the middle of the night, I sat up in bed, terrorized by a nightmare. I had dreamed that both Leah and I had been taken over by intruding malevolent spirits. We were yelling and screaming and making all kinds of noise and the manager of the motel came to quiet us down. That was not the worst part, however. What was so bad was that the entity who was bothering me in my sleep, and with whom I was somehow identified or confused, began talking to me or through me in my dream. Its wretched voice was saying, "I did *not* kill my children! It's all a mistake. I didn't do it!"

As I awoke from this horrible nightmare, I had the same cold chills and the frightened feeling in my viscera that had been experienced earlier in the night. It was a long time before I was able to get back to sleep.

I told Leah about the dream while we were dressing and packing in the morning, and we decided that all the happenings of the night must have some significance, although we had no idea what. So I sat down and wrote a complete report of the events and our reactions to them and signed my name to it. Leah attested in writing to the fact that what was said was true as it involved her and as I had reported it to her. Then she signed her name.

We left our room to go to the office and settle our bill and inquire the way to the nearby hamlet of Machiasport, where we still hoped to acquire as much information as possible about the famous early American ghost. While I was talking to the manager, Leah picked up a newspaper. Then she rushed over to me and showed me an article on the front page. It seemed to have direct application to my experience during the night, so I immediately documented the incident. I showed the manager what we had written and signed prior to coming into her office, and then asked her to sign another statement, which read as follows:

"I am witness to the fact that Miss Susy Smith has shown me an account which she had written prior to coming into my office at ten o'clock this morning. While in this office her friend discovered an article in the Tuesday, July 5, Bangor *Daily News* that she felt applied to her dream of last night." Signed, Barbara Manchester, July 5, 1966.

That newspaper article and subsequent ones we read told the tragic story of Mrs. Constance Fisher, age thirty-seven, who was being held without bail for the murder on Thursday, June 30, of her three children by drowning. Twelve years before, this same woman had drowned her first three children. She had been placed in a mental institution and had later been released to return to her husband. She had borne three more children and now had killed them also. On each occasion, Mrs. Fisher had been found unconscious beside the bathtub where the bodies of her children lay. The first time, she had written a note that read: "God told me it was the only way to save them." The note now found beside her body said: "I'm sorry to have to do this. I haven't done a proper job in raising the children. They will be better off in Heaven."

How can I explain my involvement with this case? There is the possibility, of course, that I was picking up the anguished thoughts of the imprisoned woman via telepathy. But, in that case, why was she denying killing her children? Did she perhaps realize that she might have gone into a mediumistic trance of some kind and been taken over by some invisible monster who performed the actual acts while she was unconscious? Did she by then also realize that it had not been God speaking to her, but possibly the voice of some bad spirit who was trying to cause her to perform this crime because of his very devilishness? Certainly, if it was her thoughts I was receiving, there is no explanation for the chills of the early part of the night and the presence of evil we felt in the room. I could only be sorry that poor Mrs. Fisher, apparently a good Catholic, had not been as aware as we were of the possible presence of wicked entities and how to protect herself from them. I am sure that many people in mental institutions are there because they did not realize the possibility that they might be highly sensitive to spirit influence and thus had no way to protect themselves from invasion.

So my ultimate conclusion about this horrible experience is that, rather than receiving a telepathic impression from Mrs. Fisher, by opening myself up to receptivity to spirit intrusion and by actually sending out invitations as I had done all day to the ghost of Nelly Butler, I had attracted the horrible invisible creature who was still in the neighborhood after wreaking his wrath on her. He may have been only a highly confused and miserable earthbound spirit. Perhaps he had even killed his own children when he was alive on earth. I think this entity had tried to take me over earlier in the evening, when I was willing to go into trance. After he was rebuffed, he made the effort to reach me through my dreams.

Whatever the explanation, I had certainly picked up someone's intense turmoil. It was many a long day—and night—before I stopped cringing when I recalled that agonized cry in my dream: "It's all a mistake! I didn't kill my children!"

CHAPTER XV

"Is There No End to Windy Words?"*

The results of my total hip replacement, in June 1976, were completely astounding. My surgeon, Dr. Melvin Roberts, had warned me in advance that although he was sure to be able to give me a stable hip joint, it would hardly be possible to expect those muscles that had been nearly atrophied for so long to stretch enough that he could lengthen the left leg to match the right. He thought it might be dangerous to try. But the muscles responded beautifully and did exactly what he wanted them to do, and my legs came out almost exactly even in length. Dr. Roberts and his associates all told me it was a miracle, and I thank God for it.

This was the easiest surgery I have ever undergone. I went into the operation with complete confidence in the Lord's protection, because of the promise received, was kept under sedation afterward until all the pain was eliminated, and experienced little discomfort during the entire hospitalization. In fact, I was so continuously sedated that I hardly remember eating my meals or seeing my visitors during the week that followed.

After about ten days I was home, and then the muscles that had been awry for so many years kicked up at being set straight

* Job 16:3 (New American Bible)

once again, and for over a month I was in a great deal of pain. Dr. Roberts said my X rays were "super," and there turned out to be nothing wrong that exercise in a therapeutic pool did not correct very quickly. By fall I was bouncing along blithely with one cane and the promise that even that would soon be discarded. And now, both my legs being of equal length, the built-up shoe is gratefully and happily a thing of the past.

During the time the muscles were hurting so much, someone asked me why I did not appeal to Jesus to remove my suffering, as had successfully been done with my arm the year before. I did pray about it a good deal but realized almost immediately that the pain was trying to tell me something. We had to figure out that certain movements and exercises were pulling those sore muscles incorrectly. When they were stopped and exercise in the pool was substituted, everything was all right. If the pain had been relieved early, I would not have made a special trip to the doctor and discovered what was being done wrong.

This indicates an excellent point about prayer which I have been doing a good bit of thinking about since. Sometimes conditions are not right for a miraculous healing. Then if one requests it and does not receive it, he is likely to feel neglected by God or possibly even that he is unworthy to receive a healing.

Friends have also wondered why I underwent the surgery and did not just wait for God to repair my hip. Although there is no doubt that He could have, if I'd had enough faith or if it had seemed expedient to Him to do so, it would have been like asking Him to supplant an arm or leg that had been cut off— pretty problematical. After all, there was no real socket there and no head to the femur. So it would have been a replacement job of such a high order that it was hard to bring myself to believe it likely.

I do expect the Lord to heal my arthritis and am trying to get the proper mental attitude about it so that He can do it with a minimum of resistance from my subconscious mind. Until He does, I thank Him for it every day. How much better it is to have arthritis than, say, Parkinson's disease or multiple sclerosis! I praise the Lord for my infirmities!

And now that this book is practically finished, I reflect on what it may accomplish. Have I, in the proper way, told about my lifetime search for understanding so that others can identify with it and perhaps be helped by reading of my struggles? Can my report of my growth through a variety of concepts up to Christianity assist any readers to achieve better conclusions? Certainly some of you probably have had some of the same complications and complaints. Perhaps even a too ardent child-ish belief in Santa Claus, followed by ultimate disillusionment, may have caused you to become critical of other things you believed in. I am sure a great many of you gave up all religion in college, as I did. So many professors today are materialists, behaviorists, atheists, or agnostics that it takes a mighty strong childhood faith to withstand their cynicism.

As far as my twenty-some years of researching in the psychic field is concerned, nothing like this may have been undertaken by many of my readers. But then again, perhaps it has and they realize, with the Harrisons and me, that there are many closed doors along that route. My good experiences with the psychic field opened some doors, but not wide enough. It was not until I had the Baptism in the Holy Spirit that I truly found inner happiness. If this book has turned away even a few who were flirting with the occult, I will be grateful. If it has turned away many more, I will be overjoyed, and I know He who inspired me to write it will be too.

How may we conclude, then, that one ought to be a Christian? In part, says Hans Küng, in *On Being a Christian*, because the other choices are inadequate. This is exactly what has been discovered in my case. Having studied, or at least looked at, a variety of gods of various other religions, I have learned that only Jesus' God—"a glorious Father" satisfies my requirements.

As Küng says, the test of being a Christian "is not assent to this or that dogma . . . but the acceptance of faith in Christ and imitation of Christ."

This could not be more true. One quickly learns that it simplifies his life if he attempts to live as Jesus would have lived and to think as Jesus would have thought. Any effort to emulate Him is progress in character development. St. Paul puts it this way (Ephesians 4:13 and 15, Good News): ". . . we shall become mature men, reaching to the very height of Christ's full stature. . . . by speaking the truth in a spirit of love, we must grow up in every way to Christ. . . ."

I find this particularly applicable in respect to my fault-finding nature. When my instinct to evaluate someone critically comes to the fore and I find myself thinking something caustic, I try to remember to say to myself, "Jesus would not have judged him that way. He would have loved him in spite of it." And then I look for lovable things in the person. They can always be found. As the old lady said about the bad boy, "Well, he kin whistle good."

Another place where this is helpful is in assuaging hurt feelings. Someone may have done something to make me feel momentarily rejected. There have been times in the past when such a thing could have been built up into a real problem. Now I say, "Jesus would love him in spite of this and overlook it completely. And so must I." The hurt is gone immediately, and the problem is never dwelt on again. And usually it is discovered that the slight was not intended in the first place, so all the worry would have been for nothing.

Franciscan priest Rev. Augustine Milon said on the "700 Club" in the winter of 1977, "To accept Jesus in His Holy Spirit is a challenge. And to live up to it is also a challenge."

So the answer to "Why be a Christian?" is "Because it works!" My personal experience convinces me that if you become a spirit-filled Christian it works even better. And, as Father Milon says, it is even more of a challenge.

As I think back over the many paths I investigated before arriving at the point in my development where I now find myself, an analogy comes to mind:

Imagine a great river which is God, or the flowing energy of

God which is our contact with Him. How do various individuals approach this river?

The metaphysician sits on a hill overlooking this river and mentally projects himself into it.

The agnostic sees it but denies that it has anything to do with God or anything else supernormal or supernatural.

The intellectual gets a telescope and various instruments and measures the length and breadth and depth of the river, but he never goes into it.

The ordinary Christian sprinkles some of the water on himself or briefly dunks himself in it and cries, "I'm saved!" But he stays on the bank from then on.

The Christian who has had the Baptism in the Holy Spirit jumps into the waters of this river and splashes joyously about. Then he makes it a point to cavort in the river at least once every day and possibly more often. And he never drinks anything else but its refreshing, invigorating waters.

How glad I am to have finally been ready for Jesus at a time when the power of the Holy Spirit is working in the minds of many people like a fresh breeze that could sweep the world clean! With concentration on the wonderful gifts of Pentecost, on love of Jesus and one's fellow men, and on the Baptism in the Holy Spirit, the entire concept of staid, orthodox Christianity could be lightened to one of glowing spiritual happiness for all.

There is nothing like writing a book about your religious experiences to help you receive and maintain a feeling of God's glorious presence. With the hope that the reader will share a bit of this glow, I can only conclude with a resounding "Praise the Lord" for the great joy He has brought into my soul by coming into my life.

Bibliography

Aranove, Marvin. "Hebrew of the Hebrews—The Story of a Fulfilled Jew," *Full Gospel Business Men's Voice*, May 1972.

Bach, Marcus. *The Inner Ecstasy*. Nashville: Abingdon Press, 1969.

Basham, Don. *A Handbook on Tongues, Interpretation and Prophecy*. Monroeville, Pa.: Whitaker Books, 1971.

Bennett, Dennis; and Bennett, Rita. *The Holy Spirit and You*. Plainfield, N.J.: Logos International, 1971.

Dart, John; and Chandler, Russell. "Speaking in tongues: Is it all religious?" Los Angeles *Times* (Reprinted in *The Arizona Republic*, Saturday, January 24, 1976).

Flame, The, December 1976.

Frankl, Viktor, *The Unconscious God*. New York: Simon & Schuster, 1975.

Ham, Major Clarence. "Power to Conquer." In *Voices of the Military*, FGBMF I booklet, n.d.

Hill, Harold; with Harrell, Irene. *How to Live Like a King's Kid*. Plainfield, N.J.: Logos International, 1974.

Küng, Hans. *On Being a Christian*. New York: Doubleday, 1976.

Rhine, J. B. *The Reach of the Mind*. New York: William Sloane Associates, 1947.

Roberts, Oral. *Abundant Life Magazine*. October 1976. Tulsa, Okla.: Oral Roberts Evangelistic Association, Inc.

——. *Seed-Faith Commentary on the Holy Bible*. Tulsa, Okla.: Pinoak Publishers, 1975.

Robertson, Pat; with Buckingham, Jamie. *Shout It from the Housetops*. Plainfield, N.J.: Logos International, 1972.

Sherrill, John. *They Speak with Other Tongues*. New York: Pyramid, 1970.

Synan, Vinson. *Charismatic Bridges*. Ann Arbor, Mich.: Word of Life Publishers, 1974.